Worlds of Power,
Worlds of Light

Jenna's book is such a gift! This was the first book I read that really allowed me to feel what Rama was like as a teacher in the body. I recommend Worlds of Power, Worlds of Light *to my meditation students, especially if they're interested in learning more about Rama.*

~Natalie Dane

Fabulous Spiritual Journey!
This is a fascinating tale of a personal spiritual journey with an enlightened American Buddhist meditation teacher known as Rama. I thoroughly enjoyed reading about the courageous and exciting adventures of a young woman on the path to spiritual awakening. I highly recommend this book for anyone seeking a pathway to spiritual evolvement. It is truly both powerful and filled with light.

~Ros Reynolds

This book takes you into higher states of awareness not just with yourself, but with your meditation and practice. This book will change your life!

~Hathor Reccow

The magical and fantastical journey told in this courageously honest account has inspired and intrigued me, such that my belief in what is possible has greatly expanded and my outlook on life has been forever altered for the better.

~J. Aboud

Worlds of Power,
Worlds of Light

Jenna Sundell

Electric Bliss Publishing

ISBN: 0615909345
ISBN-13: 978-0615909349 (Electric Bliss Publishing)

Special thanks to my Teacher,
Rama,
Who opened my eyes to
The wonder of Eternity.

CONTENTS

GRATITUDE

My eternal gratitude goes to Rama for taking me on these adventures so I could share the light of Enlightenment with you through this book. Rama students treasure their privacy, and most choose to reveal themselves only at certain times to specific people for the sole purpose of bringing more Light into this world. Out of respect, I will not list names in this acknowledgement of gratitude. All of you who have helped this book come into being know who you are. In case you have forgotten, here are a few reminders.

Thank you for bringing me coffee at 5am when I got up to write the first drafts before work. Much gratitude for feedback on the manuscript and for not flying into a jealous rage when you found out my unexplained disappearances involved seeing Rama outside the seminar hall. To my non-Rama student friends, you have my gratitude for your honest feedback of the manuscript and for believing in me and the book. Thank you for putting up with endless nights of me locked in my office as I struggled with rejection from publishers, endless edits, and layout and printing issues. Thank you for introducing me to countless 80's students, your enduring friendship, and for taking the teaching and publishing plunge with me. Thank you for the phone calls and emails requesting copies of the manuscript.

I have much gratitude for the event in La Jolla where I distributed and sold out of the first version of the book.

Thank you for helping me carry the stacks of photocopied books. You honored me at an event in Los Angeles when you held up my book and declared everyone should read it. This inspired a proper edition and mass distribution. Thank you to the gals who created the artwork for the cover, and to the website guru who gave us a place to meet in cyberspace and in your tiny apartment with the bunnies and birds.

Upon release and for years afterwards, thank you for all the wonderful emails complementing the book. For those of you whom I could still reach, thank you for letting me print your comments. My gratitude also goes to you who provided proofreading, editing, feedback, and support for this Anniversary edition. A big thank you to my Facebook friend whose post held the stars I had seen in my quest for a new design and whose photographic art graces the cover.

Thank you all for making this book a reality.

with love and light,
Jenna

Never be afraid to share a meditation experience, dream or vision. When you do so, you must do so without egotism – without being special.

~ Rama

PREFACE

"Rama, I know I have something important to write, but I can't figure out what it is," I said as we sat together in the Range Rover. Months earlier, I had asked him to work with me as a writer, so I began writing. Even after pages and pages, nothing held my interest. The spark simply wasn't there, and I was stumped.

"You really don't know?" asked Rama incredulously. He looked at me as if I had just eaten a box of crayons.

"No, I don't. I keep writing, but nothing's working," I whined with my eyes down. "I keep starting stories, but none of them feel right. I know there's something that needs to be written, but I'm stuck."

Shaking his head, he finally said, "The Study. You need to write about the Study."

"I can do that?" I asked. "Really?" I knew one day I would write about the teachings, but I felt nowhere near ready.

Rama gave me that look again.

"Well, yeah." he said. "But the book is not about you. It's about the Study. You should write it from the perspective of someone who doesn't know anything about meditation."

"O.K." I said as the enormity of this task began to sink into my mind.

"So the book is not about you. Remember that," he said, making eye contact with me. "It's not about you, it's about the Study."

During the following week, my ego exploded. Rama had asked me to write about the Study! I felt exhilarated and began writing during every spare minute.

At the next seminar, Rama brought up the subject of writing and asked those who were interesting in writing about the Study to stay. After the event, I looked around the room and saw about fifty people who had remained in their seats to hear what Rama had to say.

"Wouldn't it be great to have an entire shelf of books about the Study?" he asked near the end of his talk.

My ego deflated instantly. My first thought was: I need to get writing – I have to be done first. Then I stopped. I saw the excitement in Rama's eyes. I knew he was right. It really would be cool to have an entire shelf of books about the study of Enlightenment as taught by Rama.

From that conversation, this little book was born. None of the characters represent real people. They are composites of people I met along the way, and I have used artistic license to simplify the story and events. Even Rama as portrayed here is merely my perception of him. There is no way to convey all Rama is through words. Instead, I have attempted to provide an introduction to him and the teachings of Enlightenment.

Rama read many early versions of this story. Once he finished, flashes of inspiration would fill my mind, and the next version took shape. We worked together for several years in this unconventional fashion. This created a strong internal bond between us, which I suspect is the real reason he worked with me on this project, just as he worked on different projects with other students.

When word about the existence of this book got out, students contacted me begging for copies. Since I had been unable to find a publisher, the first version consisted of photocopies bound together. The book was an instant hit, and I knew it deserved to be formatted as a real book. I released the first proper edition in 2001, as Jenna Walsh before I was married, through Xlibris, one of the first print on-demand companies. As of this writing, that version is still available through their website.

Fifteen years later, with requests for the book still coming in, I decided to make it easier to find by releasing it under my married name. Part of me wanted to perform a complete makeover; however it felt more appropriate to protect the integrity of the original book. I restrained myself to only very light editing to make the story easier to read.

Over the years, many other students have written and shared their books and experiences. This is my book about the Study: simple, sweet, and told by someone who really didn't know anything at the beginning of her journey. While it is a fast read, please know there is much packed into the pages. I encourage you to read it several times to discover all it has to offer. As Rama requested, this book is not about me; it is about the Study. Everything you need to know to get started with your own practice is in these pages. So please, enjoy the journey into Light!

THE DOOR OPENS

No iron chain, or outward force of any kind,
could ever compel the soul of man to believe or disbelieve.
- Carlyle

The tears came, and this time I didn't think they would ever stop. I walked slowly, carefully stepping over the fallen branches up to my hidden rock next to the waterfall. Sunbeams sparkled on the ripples in Stow Lake like tiny passengers traveling with the flow of the water. The image of that red-headed tramp from the liquor store wearing my robe at Larry's house kept flashing in my mind.

When I opened the door, I heard them laughing and thought nothing of it, until I saw Larry's hand on her bare leg and her breasts hanging out of my robe. The silk one with the embroidered dragon that Larry had given me for Christmas. It was the nicest piece of clothing I owned and now I never wanted to see it or him again.

He looked at me with his big brown eyes as if to say he was sorry. My whole body turned to ice as I said, "I stopped by to get my sociology book, but I guess I'll take them all." I left the key on the kitchen table.

On my way to the park, I ran into Katey at the bus stop on Geary Boulevard. She was on her way to the Oakland airport to meet Tara and the other students from her meditation class. When she told me she was going to Los Angeles to meet Rama, Tara's teacher, I tried to talk her out of going. She had met Tara only a few weeks earlier, and I was worried that Larry would be right. Anytime he had seen an advertisement for a spiritual study group, he would lecture me about how those people were out to rip off anyone who showed the least bit of interest. Something in my gut told me he was wrong, but I didn't want to lose Katey to some weird cult.

I watched a bird glide over the lake and land in a tree as I thought about Katey's reply, that I had no right to put down something I knew nothing about. Another tear slipped down my cheek as I realized that on top of losing Larry, I had blown my chance to learn anything more about her meditation class. Even though Larry had jaded my opinion of meditation, I was curious about it, especially after seeing Katey. She had just finished her degree at San Francisco State University, and now she was earning a certificate in computer programming. Her excitement about life made me jealous, and losing Larry made it almost too much to bear. Her bus came before I had a chance to tell her it was over between me and Larry, and I didn't know when I would run into her again.

I dried my tears, heaved my over-stuffed backpack onto my shoulder and walked home to the flat in the Richmond district I shared with two other students from San Francisco State University. The guys had their own lives, and for the first time I was glad I didn't have to talk to them, that we were only roommates and not friends. If anyone had asked me what was wrong, I knew the tears would start flowing all over again.

I wanted to talk to Tanya about Larry, but she was still in Hawaii and wouldn't be back until the end of the summer. Tanya had been right all along about Larry. Repeatedly she had warned me about how he liked to play around and he was just using me to show off at the clubs with a pretty girl on his arm. The more I thought about it, the evidence became clear. He would show up late or cancel our dates with no explanation, and then show up the next day at the bank where I worked with a half dozen roses. The long talks about his strange disappearances always ended with me feeling like I had pushed him away, that it was somehow my fault that he didn't show. Now I knew the truth: Larry wasn't ready for a serious relationship and there was nothing I could do to change him.

With Katey gone to Los Angeles and Tanya in Hawaii for the summer, I pulled myself together as the sun sank into the ocean and went to the Abbey Tavern to find my old bar buddies. Tom and Jack were still there, sitting on the same bar stools as nearly a year ago when I first met Larry. Together we drowned my sorrows and had a good drunken laugh about my latest failed attempt to find Mr. Right. Larry had hated hanging out at the Abbey Tavern, and that night I finally understood why. Tom and Jack were still doing the same thing they had been doing for the past five years: working all day and drinking all night to numb the pain of dying dreams. I stumbled home alone, knowing in my drunken stupor that there had to be more to life than selling my time for a few dollars and sitting in a beer-soaked bar all night.

Tanya returned from Hawaii with stories about Sufi dancers and a yearning to find some way to touch the spirit she had felt on the island. She was the last person I expected to have a spiritual awakening. I knew her best from the Abbey Tavern and her incredible ability to drink anyone under the table and still make it to class on time the next day. She kept me inspired about school by embracing the debate team and using her skills to talk me into going another year, even though some days I felt a degree in Sociology wouldn't do me any good in the real world. In my heart, I knew I was using school to stop me from giving up on life and becoming a full-time bar fly. All I really wanted to do was write stories while watching the ocean crash against the coast, but that was just a fairy tale in my mind. My parents and teachers taught me there were bills to pay, that I needed a real job and maybe when I retired I could write for fun.

Tanya started searching for a meditation class to join, and dragged me to one group after another. The people we met talked about love and peace, but none of them seemed to be very loving or peaceful. Once the lecture ended, the cliques would form, excluding the newcomers from the community they preached about. Finally I told her I had enough of the hypocrisy and went back to spending my nights either scribbling poetry in my tattered notebook or drinking in the bar with Jack and Tom.

A few weeks after the fall semester started, Tanya met a meditation teacher who was another one of Rama's students. She and Katey talked about the energy they felt at the classes, and laughed at jokes I didn't get as we ate lunch together at the diner on Geary Boulevard. They seemed too happy to be real; twice I asked them what kind of drugs they were on, but they insisted they were just blissing from meditation.

"So why don't you go with me to Tara's class on Saturday," asked Katey as I watched a gorgeous blond man walk across the street. "That is, if you can stop thinking about sex long enough," she added with a laugh.

Reluctantly, I agreed to check it out.

On Saturday, Katey arrived with the afternoon fog as it spilled over Seal Rock and began creeping through the Richmond district towards my flat. We escaped over the Golden Gate Bridge and headed to Marin, where the sun was still shining. I asked Katey about Tara and the meditation class, but Katey refused to talk about her or the class. With a big smile, she told me I would just have to wait and see for myself.

The musty odor of the Unitarian Church enveloped us as I closed the wooden door, blocking out the afternoon sun. Katey and I had arrived at the meditation class before anyone else, so we wandered around looking at the yellowing pictures on the walls. As the faces of elderly priests stared back at me, I thought to myself, why are we in a church? I thought they only taught about Christianity here, not meditation.

The wooden cross above the alter reminded me of my grandmother's church, and the earthy smell made me think of the basement where Sunday School was taught. I hated sitting in that little room, with the rich kids who waved their dollar bills when it was time to put our donations in the collection plate. I could still see the disappointment on Ms. Clark's face when I pushed my pennies towards her.

As the minutes passed, I wished that no one would show up so we could go hiking on Mount Tamalpais instead of sitting in this stuffy church listening to a lecture about meditation.

Two other students arrived with a stack of leaflets advertising the class. Katey introduced me to Sarah and John, and told me they had been studying with Tara for several months. John explained they had just been out on the main road in front of the boutiques attempting to recruit people, but without much luck. When I noticed they were both wearing chinos and polo shirts like Katey's, I began to wonder if this was another cookie-cutter operation where everyone dressed and talked the same.

Standing next to them in my ripped jeans and threadbare jacket, I knew I looked like a beggar hoping for a handout. I was used to blending in with the hippies on Haight Street, but in this church I felt out of place. For the first time in my life, not having the money to buy nice clothes bothered me.

The tapping of Tara's shoes on the wooden floor echoed through the room, commanding the attention of the others. Katey, Sarah, and John turned to greet her with wide smiles, slightly bowing their heads in greeting. I watched her critically; she didn't look like any spiritual teacher I had ever seen. With her pressed blouse and gray slacks she looked more like a yuppie at work on a casual Friday than someone who was into meditation.

After welcoming the others, Tara turned her dark eyes towards me. "Have you ever meditated before?" she asked sweetly, flashing a smile. Her short brown hair framed her face like a china doll, emphasizing her small frame.

"Not really, but I've read a few books," I replied, wondering what this business woman could possibly know about spirituality. I had been to a few New Age classes around the Bay Area, and none of the teachers had shown up wearing business clothes like this woman.

"Oh, that's nice," she said curtly, seeming to dismiss me. She turned to the others waiting patiently behind her. "Since there's only us, let's go on a hike. I think we can all fit in my car."

Tara led the way. As soon as I saw that she drove a Mercedes I was convinced this group was more into money than spirituality. She was probably just another charlatan who would do a few mind reading tricks and then ask for a donation. I had already met enough people who claimed that they could save me with their religion, if only I paid them first. Since I was Katey's guest, I kept my thoughts to myself and climbed into the back seat.

Tara sped up the mountain, following the

curves with precision through the thick layer of fog typical of Northern California. At least she's a good driver, I thought to myself, as I tried to stop cutting her down in my mind. From the top of the mountain, I could make out the San Francisco skyline beneath the mist settling in the valley. We walked behind Tara at a quick pace, and I silently began scrutinizing every move she made. Nothing she did seemed right to me. I had decided she was a phony and there was no way to convince me otherwise.

We stopped at a large boulder on top of the peak, where Tara asked us to sit with our backs straight. "Close your eyes and focus," she commented. "If you have any thoughts, just ignore them."

With closed eyes, she led us through a short meditation. When we focused on the heart, I felt a strange tingle in my hands and chest. I ignored the sensation, and continued to try to stop thinking, as Tara had suggested. No matter how hard I tried to quiet my mind, I kept thinking about how stupid we must all look, sitting on top of a rock with our eyes closed. In my mind, I imagined what Larry would say if he could see me. When I had just started to relax, Tara ended the meditation and everyone bowed. I opened my eyes and looked around; the others were all smiling for some reason that I didn't understand.

"Now let's practice seeing," said Tara. "Don't focus on anything in particular; just gaze out over the trees and clouds."

I stared out at the fog covering the horizon, and I began to notice an odd stream of colors. Thinking my contacts must be dirty, I blinked my eyes repeatedly to clear them and then gazed into the trees below us. The pine trees blended together into a smear of green and brown. Suddenly, a huge American Indian in full headdress appeared at the base of the hill. My jaw dropped as I admired how he towered over the trees like a tribal shaman from a movie. I looked down at my hands to get myself back into reality, but when I gazed back at the trees he was still there, with black-tipped feathers streaming down his back from his headdress. Lines of blue and red war paint decorated his face and a beaded leather vest covered his chest. I watched him surveying the horizon for what seemed like hours, until Tara broke the silence, asking us what we had seen.

I wanted to burst in to ask if they had seen the Indian, but when I looked again, he was gone. Only the shadows of the trees remained at the bottom of the mountain. It must have been my imagination, I thought, trying to convince myself. The others all said they had seen various colors and geometric shapes in the clouds as I debated whether or not to admit that I had seen an Indian hanging out in the trees. No one else mentioned it, so I was sure they would think I was lying or just plain crazy.

"So how about you," Tara asked, "did you see anything?" She looked at me as if she expected me to say no, or to just agree with the others.

"Well," I answered, as a thought struck me that I really didn't care what anyone thought of me, "when I was gazing into the trees, I saw a huge Indian."

"How tall was he?" asked Tara with genuine

interest. "Like if he was standing next to you."

Surprised, I looked up into the sky next to me, imagining the Indian standing there. "About twenty or thirty feet, I suppose," I answered, trying not to feel foolish talking about daydreams as if they were real.

"It sounds like you saw a guardian. There are beings who protect the forests," she explained to the group, reminding me of a mythology teacher. "They usually hang out near the edges of the forest and drive people away with their energy. If you've ever walked around the woods at night and felt like you shouldn't be there, you probably felt one of them."

My eyes grew wide with shock as she explained the vision. I opened my mouth to ask her if she had seen him, but she stood up to leave before I could get a word out.

"It's time to go," finished Tara, dropping the subject.

I watched Tara with renewed respect as we followed her down the path to the car. After hearing her talk about the Indian, I realized maybe there was something that she could teach me.

In front of the church, Tara handed me a tape by a band named Zazen. "Listen to this when you meditate; my teacher, Rama, produced the music," she said as she moved a suitcase back into place. "I'll see you in a couple of weeks. I have to go catch a plane back to my client in Boston."

"You flew out here just to teach this class?" I asked. No successful business woman would fly across country just to teach a meditation class.

"Yeah, it happens. Sometimes things come up that try to get in the way," she answered, shrugging her shoulders. "There's more to meditation than just sitting with your eyes closed."

At home, I listened to the tape Tara had given me and attempted to still my thoughts like we did on the mountain. From my bedroom, I heard my roommates joking as they climbed the stairs to our flat. Suddenly, I became very self-conscious and wondered what they would say if they knew I was meditating. I couldn't stop thinking about them, so with a sigh of frustration I turned off the tape. From out of nowhere, a voice popped in my head and said I would be moving soon. I whipped my head around, expecting to see someone standing there, when I realized it was just a passing thought. But I like this flat, I laughed to myself, amazed at how loud everything seemed now that I had turned off the tape.

When I saw Katey a few days later, I made a joke about the voice telling me I was going to move.

"Oh, you probably felt your roommates, and your subtle body knows you can't live with them and meditate," she said matter-of-factly, pulling her long blond hair into a ponytail as we walked down the beach.

"What do you mean? My subtle body – what's that?" I had heard the term before, but was never quite sure what it meant.

"When you start to meditate, you become more sensitive, especially to other people. And your subtle body is, I guess, like the energy surrounding your physical body that feels stuff. It's kind of hard to explain, but you've heard of aura readings, right?"

"Yeah. So the subtle body is like your aura? Will I be able to see colors around people like a fortune teller?" I teased, thinking of all the ads I had seen for psychics and palm readers.

"Maybe," retorted Katey, raising an eyebrow. "I guess it depends on how well you can see. I heard one of the older student's third eye opened, and now she can see people's past lives. That would be really cool if I could do that."

"The third eye," I asked, touching my forehead. "That's this spot between my eyebrows, right?"

"Uh huh," said Katey, looking out over the Pacific Ocean. "Wow, it's so clear out today. I wish I could stay out here forever."

"Yeah, me too. But," I said glancing at my watch, "I need to stop at the library before my sociology class."

I walked up the hill to Sunset Boulevard and caught the bus back to San Francisco State University, still thinking about all this weird meditation stuff. None of the books I had read described a vision as intense as the Indian I had seen on the mountain, and the way Tara spoke about it as if it were an everyday occurrence confused me. The Castaneda books I had read described some awesome events, but long ago I had decided they were just drug-induced hallucinations. I wanted to believe what I had seen was real, but it was so far-fetched I couldn't even tell my buddies at the bar. They would ask what kind of drugs I was on, and then make wisecracks all night.

Nevertheless, I meditated every morning and night, hoping it could somehow make my life better.

My routine of school, work, bar just wasn't fun anymore. I enjoyed working at the bank and filling in at the college bookstore, but lately it seemed like I would be trapped forever as a bank teller. And the more I thought about school, the less certain I felt that I should be studying sociology. I had started taking philosophy classes too, but I had no idea what I would do with my degree or when I would finish. Katey had already graduated with a speech major, and now with Tara's help, she was earning her certificate at Computer Learning Center. I wasn't interested in computers like Tara or her students, but after seeing that Indian on Mount Tamalpais, I knew there had to be more to life than just college and work.

MEETING THE MASTER

*Humility does not consist in hiding our talents and virtues,
in thinking ourselves worse and more ordinary than we are,
but in possessing a clear knowledge of all that is lacking in us
and in not exalting ourselves for that which we have.*

                                                        -Lacordaire

When Tara came back to town, Katey drove me to see her at Fort Mason, a collection of buildings near the Marina where people rented rooms to teach public classes. Although the first class had snagged my interest in meditation, I still wasn't completely sold on this whole group-study thing. In the back of my mind I kept asking myself, where's the catch? What do Tara and her teacher really want from us? The Zazen tape produced by Rama made meditation much easier than anything else I had tried, and the music was truly beautiful. But still, I had been on the streets enough times to know when someone helps you, they expect something in return.

When we entered the room, Katey introduced me to another student, Matthew. He had been studying with Tara and Rama for nearly a year and was almost finished with computer school. He had a cute smile, but he looked too much like a yuppie for my taste, with his neatly trimmed hair and pressed, button-down shirt.

"When I met Tara," explained Matthew as we waited for the class to begin, "I was working in a coffee shop, just hanging out. She took me on a hike and taught me how to meditate. Then she introduced me to Rama, and my whole life took a major jump. I can't believe I'm almost done with my computer certificate program. I've already been doing some work for Tara in Visual Basic programming, so I've got some great experience for when I go looking for a job."

The way he kept rambling on made me feel like I was listening to a commercial on the radio. I just smiled, and looked around at the other people in the room.

A blond-haired man sat a few chairs away from mine, but none of the regular students seemed to know who he was. I was about to say hello when Tara walked in, her arms filled with a large pillow, a bag of tapes, and a portable tape player. Matthew immediately jumped up to help plug in the tape player while Katey arranged the tapes on the side table. Together they laid out some handouts listing recommended books and information about the different chakras, or energy centers, in the body.

Wow, these kids are just like puppy dogs, I thought when I noticed them seeking Tara's approval of how they lined up the tapes and the handouts. Tara nodded towards them and placed the pillow on the table set up in front of the chairs. She removed her shoes and sat on the pillow cross-legged.

She smiled and greeted each of us by name, until her eyes met the man at the end of the row. In a polite tone, she said, "Hello. What's your name?"

"Anthony." He was a tall skinny kid with short blond hair, and seemed pretty clean-cut. *He'll fit right in*, I thought to myself as I sized him up.

"Have you ever meditated before, Anthony?" continued Tara.

"No, not really," he answered.

"Well, my name is Tara and I teach beginning meditation. You could think of it as a kindergarten class. All I do is teach the basic technique my teacher has taught me. I'm not enlightened, but I have studied meditation for a very long time, so I can answer some of your questions. And the hard questions I can ask my teacher."

She explained the technique of focusing on each of the three main chakras at the navel, the heart, and the third eye, while pushing the thoughts out of your mind. The delicate and lively music of Zazen played as images of the guys at the bar fighting over who was going to walk me home flashed in my mind. For a brief moment I could hear Larry saying I was wasting my time with this group. When we focused on the third eye, I blocked them out and I could feel my body becoming lighter. Too soon the music stopped and everyone bowed their heads. I looked around the room, and once again, everyone was smiling about some private joke I still didn't quite get.

Tara answered a few questions and ended with information about the next class. After the others left, I scanned a handout about the chakras while I waited for Tara to finish talking to Katey. When they were done, Tara looked at me and asked if I would like to meet Rama.

"Yes, definitely," I answered, surprised at my own excitement.

"Great. I'll pay for your dinner this time," she said in a business-like tone. "The seminar is at the Mark Hopkins hotel Friday night, so why don't you get a ride with Katey. Do you have something nice to wear?" she asked, looking over my tie-dyed skirt and the frayed sleeves of my sweater. "Hey, Katey, will you let her borrow something to wear to dinner if she doesn't have anything?"

"Sure," answered Katey before I could protest. Katey ignored my stunned look as she picked up the tape player and the bag of tapes.

"Oh, thanks," said Tara with a wide grin as she carried her pillow out to the parking lot.

On Friday night, I discovered the Mark Hopkins is one of San Francisco's most glorious hotels. It sits on top of Nob Hill, rising above the city lights like a castle. The 19th century architecture, with the intricate carvings on the archways, appeared like an entrance to a fairy tale land. The grand doorway towered above me; never before had I been invited to a place so magnificent.

As Katey and I turned the corner into the banquet hall, my self-confidence dropped at the sight of hundreds of elegantly dressed people. None of the weddings or other dinner parties I had attended had ever been this fancy. My long flowered skirt and cheap blazer stood out in the crowd, but I was too confused to feel embarrassed. I couldn't understand why a bunch of rich business people were attending a lecture on meditation. The overwhelming wealth of the hotel made me suspicious. I kept asking myself weren't spiritual people supposed to use their money to help the poor, not on fancy dinners? Tara's black ball gown seemed like a bit much even for this banquet room, but she was paying for my dinner, so what could I say?

Katey started off to meet the others, so I followed, listening to snatches of the conversations. I had expected to hear a roomful of miserable people looking for the answers to all of life's problems. Instead, the business people in this room were discussing one exciting project or another, smiling as if they had touched ecstasy.

Katey and I met the other students from Tara's class, and we sat down together at a table in the back of the room. I was disappointed that we were so far from the stage. I wanted to get a good look at Rama, since everyone was so excited to see him but refused to tell me anything about him when I asked. While eating dinner, we chatted about the weather and the classes some of us were taking at college. I couldn't help noticing the tension in the room; it was like waiting for a bomb to go off.

The waiters were clearing the dessert dishes when Rama strolled in, with a briefcase in one hand and a long leather coat draped over the other. Although Tara had not mentioned what he looked like, I had expected an elderly Japanese man wearing an ocher robe. Instead Rama turned out to be a middle-aged Caucasian man, just over six feet tall, with blond curly hair and dressed in an Armani suit. As he stepped onto the platform stage set up at the far end of the banquet hall, everyone turned their chairs to face him. When I turned towards him, there was a clear aisle from my chair straight to center stage.

I watched Rama closely as he crossed his legs into the lotus position. A grace and ease accompanied his motions, as if he had performed this ritual thousands of times. My gaze kept returning to his eyes. I was positive I had never seen him before, but there was something about him that was strangely familiar.

"Tonight I'd like to talk with you about reincarnation," said Rama, as a mischievous grin crossed his face, reminding me of the Cheshire cat from *Alice in Wonderland*. "The good news is we live forever. And the bad news is, we live forever." Rama looked around at the smiles in the audience, and began again with a more serious tone.

"Life is the joining of the infinite and the finite. The eternal part of us appears in the physical world, has experiences, and then the physical part falls away when we die. While in the body, the spirit plays out its karma. That is, it continues to follow the patterns of its previous lives, changing and growing until the body dies.

"At death, the material world falls away and the spirit takes a break. The spirit takes with it the awareness it has gained during the life experience. Whatever we become conscious of becomes embedded into our nature, and those skills carry from life to life."

I relaxed in my chair, forgetting about my

23

appearance for the first time that evening. I took a sip of my coffee as I concentrated on his words.

"For example, if you studied karate in a past life, you would probably be drawn to study it in this life. In the beginning, you would have to relearn the basics. Once you had the basics down, you would tap into your past life knowledge and you would progress much faster than someone who was new to the study of karate.

"The same is true in the study of self-discovery," he continued, closing his eyes as his melodious voice spread through the room. "When you increase your awareness through meditation, or expand your consciousness through self-discovery, that knowledge travels with you from life to life. Karma propels us to continue with the actions we began in the previous moments. So most of you here have studied meditation in previous lives. By picking up the study again in this life, you can very quickly get back to where you left off and start exploring new areas.

"The process of reincarnation is very similar to going to school," explained Rama, glancing around the banquet hall. "Someone in eighth grade is not any better than someone in third grade. It just means the student in eighth grade has had more experiences and hopefully knows more. In time, the third-grader will be in eighth grade. And also like school, there is a summer vacation, when the body dies and the spirit takes a break until it is born again.

"When you meditate, you may begin to remember your past lives. This generally happens to people in their twenties, but sometimes people are younger or older. It really depends on how open and aware you are. However, remembering the particulars of who you were or what you did in a previous life really isn't very important.

"Buddhists use these recollections as a way to learn how to live better today. You can't change the past; it doesn't exist anymore. So it's important not to get hung up on remembering your past lives. If you see stuff when you meditate, it's best just to ignore it. Don't let anything distract you from silencing your mind and seeking light."

Rama pulled out a pair of sunglasses from his jacket and asked us to sit up straight so we could meditate. He put on a CD by Zazen, a band he had created with some of his students, and asked everyone to focus on him.

I gazed at him with half-closed eyes, letting the music fill my ears. The people in the room disappeared, and I could feel Rama's energy inside my mind as if he was behind my forehead, in my third eye. At first, I tried to shut him out because I was afraid. I didn't really like the idea of someone in my head, even if he was a respected spiritual teacher. Rama was persistent but not intrusive; instead he became like a vapor and slipped in through the cracks. I could feel him communicating with me telepathically. There were no words, only a soothing feeling, letting me know I was not in any danger. His energy, soft and delicate like a rose petal, shone before me like a rainbow. I knew this feeling of meditation with him, and felt a deeper love for this being, this essence, than I had ever felt for anything else in life.

We bowed after the meditation, and when I

looked up, directly at Rama, he smiled back at me. From across the room his eyes sparkled like diamonds as they met mine, and I knew I would see him again as my teacher.

Two days later, I still felt as high as I did on my way home from the Mark Hopkins. I went to my favorite perch next to the waterfall in Golden Gate Park to look at the world, seemingly for the first time. Since I had started to meditate, everything had become so much brighter and clearer to me. I had never really noticed the beauty of the clouds and the trees and even the city skyline. I giggled to myself as I realized I had been walking around in a city with an endless postcard view without noticing it for years.

The waterfall flowed into Stow Lake like a silver ribbon and the water, as it danced over the rocks, produced a delicate melody that drowned out the sound of the city. It was all so breathtaking I wanted to cry and yell out to everyone – I wanted them to see what I was seeing. But I knew they wouldn't see it. Instead they would see the dirty people and dingy streets and complain about how terrible the world was. Not even my closest drinking buddies, whom I had seen almost every week for the past year, could grasp the transformation I was experiencing from meditation.

At this point in my life, I was standing in a metaphysical doorway, and once I stepped through, I knew I could not turn back. That's just how things are in the world of self-discovery. For some, ignorance is bliss, but when you become aware of the other dimensions, you cannot go back to that ignorance by denying they exist. In meditation, I caught glimpses of these other states of awareness, these other worlds. I wanted to know more, so when I came upon this opportunity I had no choice but to jump in head first.

My meditations became stronger with practice. Some days I would have wonderful visions of colors and places I had never seen, and other times it would be very deep, quiet and profound. My two roommates began to wonder about my sudden explosion of exuberance, but with my busy schedule of two jobs and a full load at school there was never any time for them to question me about it.

The vision of Rama's luminous eyes often returned to me as I began to meditate every morning and evening, catapulting me into deeper and deeper states of ecstasy. Slowly, my perception of the world began to change. Instead of reacting to the injustices of the world with unfocused anger, I found a bizarre sense of humor that allowed me to laugh at the ridiculous situations people faced every day. When my friends became angry because there were no seats on the bus, I couldn't help laughing at them. And when my professor kept the class late, I realized how foolish it would be to get mad at the teacher. Many of my classmates ruined their whole day because of that instructor. Even though I knew I would be late for my next class, I thought his righteousness that kept him going on about the ancient Egyptians was hilarious.

A week before Halloween, after a busy day at work and a long night at school, I came home exhausted. Too tired to meditate, I took a quick shower and crawled under the covers of my bed. As I lay there with my eyes closed, I could hear Zazen off in the distance. The music grew steadily louder, but I wanted to sleep, not meditate. Frustrated, I put the pillow over my head, trying to block out the music.

I felt myself moving, then something within me let loose and I seemed to be flying at an extraordinary rate. Colors, light, and shapes snapped in and out of view faster than I could process. My awareness kept shifting with greater and greater speed; I was completely out of control. I couldn't focus on anything – the images were moving by me too quickly. It was as if I had jumped onto a roller coaster that was missing the tracks at the bottom of the hill. All I wanted was to get off the ride.

I rationalized if I could shut off the music, the trip would stop. I focused all of my will on moving towards my stereo. With great effort, I pushed myself into my room, but I was still flying very fast, like a racecar skidding across an oil-slicked track. I saw my physical body lying in bed, but I was too involved with reaching my stereo to think about it. I propelled myself to my stereo, and to my horror and amazement, I flowed right into the table and stereo. I looked down and saw myself sitting on the floor with the stereo protruding through my stomach. My body was like a shadow, all light and airy. I stretched my hand to the tape player, but my fingers glided through the buttons. I had no substance, no weight to press upon the physical world.

I stared at the stereo trying to figure out how I

could turn off the music. Suddenly, I realized the stereo wasn't even turned on, and the music wasn't coming from the speakers. It was just there, all around me. I started to panic; I didn't know what to do now that I was stuck inside my stereo. I opened my mouth to cry out, and everything faded.

I came back to consciousness, lying on my bed completely dazed. The pounding of my heart thundered in my ears as I stared up at the ceiling, my eyes wide open with shock. Totally disorientated, with only the odd sensation of traveling through space to cling to, I attempted to get a grip on reality. I began running the names of friends to call through my mind, but I knew no one would be awake and sober at 2 o'clock in the morning. As I reached for the phone, I realized even if I did talk to someone, it wouldn't matter. For this adventure, I was on my own.

THE PLANES OF LIGHT

Life is unfolding like a rose
Coming to full bloom.
Petal by petal,
It opens.
Perfume scents the air,
Spreading beauty
To even those who cannot see
Its glory.

The clash and clang of my roommate washing dishes broke the silence of my meditation. It won't be long now, I thought, as I dreamed of having my own apartment. There had to be a small place somewhere in the city I could afford, I thought as I shut off the music and began to prepare for another day.

The morning fog dissipated as I walked to work at American Savings Bank. The image of Matthew's sweet smile appeared in my mind, and I remembered the twinkle in his eyes when he had first told me about Rama. His happiness reminded me of the monks from India when they talked about their guru to my philosophy class. I had no interest in becoming anyone's devotee, but Matthew's love for Rama and Tara triggered something inside me. An overpowering feeling of respect for Rama and Tara as teachers, and for myself as a student, filled me as I walked into the bank.

After work, I called Matthew to ask him if he needed help putting up posters for Tara's next meditation class. In the evening we started in the Richmond district on Clement Street near 19th Avenue. We worked our way towards little Chinatown, telling jokes to each other and giggling as the tape became tangled again and again. While laughing with him, I noticed how cute he was, and immediately pushed the thought out of my head. I didn't want to have a sexual relationship ruin the new friendship we were just beginning to build.

"That stuff is all lies and bullshit," scoffed an old man from behind Matthew's left shoulder suddenly. Matthew ignored him and continued to hang the poster for Tara's class on the telephone pole.

"Who do you kids think you are, hanging up these posters," he continued, the smell of brandy on his breath filling the air. I took a step back, overwhelmed by the odor, as Matthew turned to face him.

"You don't have to look at it, if it bothers you," replied Matthew politely.

"You're right," said the man gruffly, tearing the poster in half from the pole. "You freaks come around here and start with all this meditation bullshit. These guys are just gonna rip you off."

"Obviously you don't understand what meditation is, or how it can change your life," answered Matthew coolly, staring at the torn poster as it floated in the wind. "And you don't ever have to, unless it's something that you want to know about. But you can't stop other people from studying and learning about meditation."

The old man stared at Matthew, not sure whether to continue the argument or walk away.

"Come on, let's go," said Matthew, gently touching my arm and turning his back on the old man. We headed up Fourth Avenue to Geary Boulevard, away from the old man's muffled curses, to finish postering.

"I can't believe how angry some people are in the world. It's like they have nothing better to do than slam other people. I just don't understand why that old man had to attack us like that," I complained while taping a poster to the lamppost.

"Well, that's just it," answered Matthew, his deep green eyes drawing me in. "Some people are just angry, and the only way they know how to deal with it is to take their frustrations out on other people. What they don't realize is whatever they throw out is just going to come back. That old man probably treats everybody the way he did us, and most people probably do the same to him. So you've got all these people slamming each other all the time, and the sad thing is none of them realize what they're doing to themselves. Rama once said forgiveness is the best revenge. If you forgive the person, like that old man, then you don't go down to his level, and you won't have to feel like he does."

"Wow," I replied, cracking a smile. "I would hate to feel like that guy. Drunk and pissed off at the world – what an awful place to be."

"Yeah," said Matthew with a dreamy look in his eyes. "Sometimes I forget how life was before I met Tara and started meditating every day. A year ago, I would have gotten into a big fight with that guy. But now, I can't even imagine doing that. I mean, why? He's already in enough pain as it is."

"Maybe I'm just naive, but I don't understand why people have to get angry just because I'm interested in something they're not. I've only met Rama once, but I know I can learn a lot from him."

"Well, I hate to tell you, but there are people much worse than that old guy. People have written articles about the study and Rama, completely tearing him up. And Cult Watch has already shown up at a couple of the events to hand out propaganda saying Rama is brainwashing people."

"Really?" I replied, shocked at the idea. "That's so weird. I mean, isn't this America, the land of freedom of religion? What's Cult Watch, anyway?"

"They're a network of people who have decided to do battle against anyone they think is involved in a cult. They've gone after other spiritual groups too. Basically, they try to destroy any religious group that isn't mainstream – which pretty much means Christianity is the only thing they accept," said Matthew.

"If they want to practice Christianity, that's great. But I don't understand why they feel the need to interfere with other people's practices. If you really get down to it, all the religions I've heard about in my philosophy classes all say the same thing. They use different words and rituals, but at the core, Truth is still Truth."

"It would be nice if everyone thought that way." replied Matthew with a laugh. "Let's go get a slice of pizza, and then I have to call it a night. I've got class in the morning, and I promised Tara I'd work on some code for her product."

"You're really into that computer stuff, huh?" I asked, wondering how such a cute guy wound up with such a geeky job. Exposing my desire to be the perpetual student, I continued, "I like studying sociology and philosophy, but I don't know what I'll do when I'm finished with my degree. Maybe I'll keep going and get my master's degree too."

"Why don't you take some computer classes? It's really cool when you start understanding how it all works. And it's so much better than having to wait on people like that guy back there all day in a coffee shop."

"Me? Take computer classes?" I said, laughing at the thought of it. "I just started learning the word processor at the college library because I can't stand my typewriter anymore, and WordPerfect is plenty for me. I can't imagine myself staring at a computer screen all day. Typing a paper on one is bad enough, with all those weird functions keys you have to know. If it wasn't for the print out of the help screen, I'd be totally lost."

"It's great when you have a problem you have to figure out. It's like doing puzzles all day. I love it. But to tell you the truth, I never expected to work with computers either. I could teach you Windows. It's really easy, just give me a call."

Matthew dropped me off at my house, and waved before turning home. I fell asleep thinking about him, trying to talk myself out of being attracted to him.

❀ ॐ ❀

Later that week, a pale yellow moon hung low in the sky as I strolled across the University campus. I smiled as I drew a deep breath of cool, crisp autumn air. I looked up at the stars and thought, I love this time of year.

I stopped in my tracks, shocked at what I had just said to myself. Then, self-conscious of standing in the middle of campus for no apparent reason, I began to walk again without looking around. During the past few years, I had hated the fall with its bitter wind and short days. But now, I felt like a kid again, when autumn was the best time of year with leaves to play in and a bite of chocolate cake on my birthday. This time, I had no expectations for the next year of my life. I was turning twenty-two and had no plans for my birthday except Tara's meditation class. Although I couldn't see very far down the road in front of me, I did know I wanted to follow it.

My birthday was on Saturday, so I spent the day before meditation class looking at apartments. My roommates were unhappy to see me leave our flat, but there was no way I could continue my meditation practice with them in the house. As I traveled around the city by bus, I started to feel slightly ill. The ride back to my house seemed to take forever, and I caught myself becoming annoyed by the people on the bus. A large woman standing in the aisle bumped me with her packages every time the bus turned a corner, and an old man stared at me as if I had two heads. I didn't speak to any of them, but I could feel their presence as if they were all sitting an inch away from me. I was being suffocated and all I wanted was to get off the bus before I went completely crazy. As I stared out the window at the stucco houses, I finally understood this feeling was what Katey had been talking about when she told me my subtle body could detect my roommates. At that moment, I could feel everyone on that bus, along with all the pain in their lives.

That evening after class, Tara threw a birthday party for me at her house. They sang a super-fast version of "Happy Birthday," and then we ate cake and ice cream. To top it off, she gave me an Zazen poster as a gift from the group. I had never been one to celebrate my birthday; too many childhood disappointments had made me cynical. To me, it was just another day, but that night Tara and the students made it a fun and special time.

After everyone else had left, Tara invited me and Katey to see Rama in Los Angeles on Monday. I thought about the unfinished paper that was already late and the mid-term exam I had to take the day after the event, but something inside me wouldn't let me say no. Seeing Rama again would be the best birthday present anyone could give me, and I knew it.

As Katey and I prepared to leave, Tara gave me a ball gown to wear.

"I don't wear it anymore, and I think it will fit you," she said, holding the peach-colored dress up in front of me.

"You mean you don't want it back?" I asked, feeling like Cinderella. The lace and silk gown must have come from an expensive store like Saks 5th

Avenue. I couldn't believe she was giving away something so beautiful.

"No, you can keep it. But you should share it," she added, nodding towards Katey.

At home that night, I called Southwest Airlines to check the fares. They had a two-for-one special, so I made plans with Katey to fly down just for the night. The hours before the seminar raced by, and before I knew it, I was sitting in the Gold Room at the Four Seasons Hotel, the finest banquet hall in Beverly Hills.

Rama was walking around, stopping at every table. When he came to our table, he smiled and said, "Tara's a real bitch, huh?"

We all looked at him in shock, not saying a word. I glanced at Tara to see her reaction, and I was even more surprised to see her smiling in agreement.

"No, you don't understand," continued Rama. "That's a compliment. You can't be a pushover in the business world. Tara's a bitch, cold and strong, and that's why she's doing so well. Because she's a woman, people expect her to get all emotional about things and not have the power to delegate authority and follow through on her ideas. But that's not the case, is it?"

"No, it's not," answered Tara as she met his eyes from her seat.

"See, if you're nice and give everybody what they want all the time, you'll get eaten alive out there. In business, people don't care about you. They're out to get the best deal at any cost, and if you let them, they'll walk all over you. So you've got to be tough, right?" he asked with enthusiasm, looking directly at Katey.

"Right," replied Tara with a grin, while the rest of us nodded in agreement.

I was still bewildered by this interaction when he walked away. To hear Rama talking about business confused me. I thought he was a spiritual teacher, not some corporate leader. And I couldn't believe he had been so blunt about Tara being tough, but at the same time, I had seen enough at my own jobs to know he was right about the cut-throat business world.

On stage, Rama spoke in the same direct, to the point fashion as he had discussed the business world with us at the table. His commitment to teaching meditation kept me hanging on every word. He didn't need to endorse anyone or any certain faith, he just told it like it was, plain and simple. The concepts he presented struck a chord of truth within me. I didn't need proof or credentials; everything he said seemed like common sense.

"Tonight we're here to discuss self-discovery," said Rama from the small stage. "As a yoga teacher, it's my job to teach you techniques that allow you to explore the hidden realms of light within your own mind. It's up to you to do the work, to put these ideas into practice. You have to understand all of the real important answers to life's questions lie within your own mind. All a teacher can do is point the way. You're the one who has to actually walk that path.

"Since everyone is unique, one technique is not sufficient for everyone. There's no set formula that says if you follow a, b, and c you'll reach Enlightenment. I have a very eclectic approach to self-discovery in that I draw from Hindu, Buddhist, and Taoist teachings. The real trick to self-discovery is to find what works for you. And the most important thing I can tell you as a yoga teacher is to be true to yourself," continued Rama.

"Many of you have not been exposed in this lifetime to the study of meditation. For this reason, I strongly recommend you go out and explore the teachers available to you. This month your assignment, should you decide to accept it, is to go visit a monastery, or attend a meditation class taught by one of the hundreds of teachers out there. My style of teaching doesn't work for everyone, so I feel it's important you go out and see for yourself the other methods of self-discovery."

Rama then began answering questions from the audience. When he addressed the person who asked a question, it was as if they were alone in the room. At times I felt I was eavesdropping, even though the room was filled with over two hundred people. Then he would say something that was so pertinent to my life, it was as if I had asked the question.

"Would you talk about dreams and what we can do on the dream plane?" asked a young woman when Rama pointed to her.

"The dream plane is just another dimension in the astral, and going there is just like going to another country. Some places are nicer than others, but just like traveling here, it takes energy to move around.

"As far as doing things, you don't have enough power yet to really do anything, except maybe get yourself trashed out. You have to remember you're the same person there as you are here, except you're traveling in a foreign country. It's easy to wind up in low energy situations in a place unfamiliar to you, especially if you've been drawn to that in the past. That's why it's a good idea to take a shower in the morning before you meditate. Water washes off the astral energy that can leave you feeling spaced out."

I began to notice a faint glow around Rama's body as he spoke. I blinked my eyes, trying to clear my vision, certain my contacts were dried out from the air-conditioning. Remembering my strange experience of falling into my stereo, I tried to focus on everything he said, despite the golden haze filling the room.

"But personally, I prefer to sleep," continued Rama. "There's really not anything that exciting in the astral. It's the planes of light, beyond the astral, where the real magic takes place. Light transforms you. Light is what changes your awareness."

We then meditated with him, listening to Zazen. I caught glimpses of light and colors, but my thoughts kept weighing down on me. Distracted by my worries about tests and late papers, I realized I was spacing out, and I became frustrated by the fact that I wasn't meditating. In my mind, I scolded myself for not concentrating harder. A moment later, we bowed and Rama said we should take a break.

On my way back to the table from the ladies' room, I noticed a long line of people waiting to ask Rama personal questions. He was still sitting on the small stage he had been on all night. I was amazed by his patience and willingness to help all those who approached him. There were so many things I wanted to ask him, but once I entered the banquet hall, none of the details of my life seemed very important. Even my strange experience of astral travel no longer seemed worthy of his concern. Somehow I knew to live in the magical world he was part of, I would have to start figuring out the answers myself.

At my table, I wondered what his life was like, what he saw when he looked at his students, and just how he managed to do all of the things he did without falling down from pure exhaustion. After hearing him talk about his music group, Zazen, and the software companies he ran, to know he was teaching in seven different cities across the United States completely amazed me. There were so many things I wanted to do with my life, but I had never followed through on any of them. I had to admit to myself even college was starting to bore me. It seemed like most of the people in the room were working with computers, but there was no way I was going to jump on that bandwagon.

I wanted to understand this incredible sensation of peace and control I felt after meditating. As I watched him on stage answering question after question, I knew Rama was willing to take the time to teach me about this mystery. I was so happy to be in that room, and only wished that I knew how to meditate more deeply, so I could see things the way I imagined he did.

"Rama," inquired a young man after the break, "How can I meditate better? I keep getting lost in my thoughts." I smiled at the question, thankful I wasn't the only person having trouble.

"Focus," he answered, pounding his fist into his

palm for emphasis. "You have to use your will power to pull your mind back and focus harder on the chakra. When you can't focus on the chakra anymore, listen to the music. Don't half-listen like it's a song on the radio, but listen to every note with your full attention. I go through the music I produce for my students with my aura, so it has the pure energy of Enlightenment in it. If you go into it with your whole being, it will take you to the planes of light.

"Meditation is stopping thought by focusing on doorways into other dimensions, and traveling into those dimensions," he continued. "One of those doorways is the chakra we focus on when we meditate. By stopping thought, you pull up the kundalini, which is the dormant energy at the base of the spine in the first chakra. When the kundalini rises, it brings you to a higher state of awareness where it is easier to focus. So every time your mind wanders, and for a while it will wander, just pull it back to your focal point. Forget about where you were and focus on being here right now."

"I wish I had known that earlier," replied the man, voicing my exact thoughts.

"Don't worry, you'll get another chance in a few minutes before I send you home," answered Rama with a playful smile.

This time when we meditated, I vowed to push myself harder than I ever had. Rama said we would meditate for two songs, and we should watch him. I locked my attention on my third eye and let the music take me where it would.

At first, I closed my eyes and I could see the dark blue silhouettes of the other students, but not

Rama's silhouette. I pushed harder, diving into the music. I opened my eyes, and a golden light filled the room. I couldn't see anything except brilliant gold and white light. My body became an empty glass figure, overflowing with liquid golden light. My head felt as if it was expanding, and my thoughts were silent. My entire being melted into the light. I was no longer there in the room – I was everywhere, one with the light. There was no scene of people before me. I had dissolved into my surroundings and became part of everything and everyone. Effortlessly, I simply flowed with the ocean of light in every direction.

I left the banquet hall feeling clear and detached, my feet barely touching the ground. Nothing was as solid as it had appeared before the seminar. During the meditation, I had reached a new level of awareness that altered my view of reality forever. The idea there is more to life than all of this physical matter was no longer just an idea; it was a plane of reality within my grasp.

I felt so complete at that moment, as if I had found the missing key that unlocked a door hidden within myself. There was nothing I wanted except to stay in that feeling of ecstasy forever. I couldn't quite grasp how deeply Rama had moved me that evening, but I knew my perception of life was changing and opening new opportunities I never could have imagined before I met him.

Katey, Matthew, Sarah, and I changed out of our formal dress and met in Tara's room to discuss the event. We all shared our experiences, highlighting our most profound moment. I had trouble describing what I had experienced, mainly because it was somehow more than an experience. Rama had transformed me into pure light. I, in the normal sense of the pronoun, didn't exist at that time, so "I" didn't really experience anything, except maybe what some would label "unity with the Divine." Everyone nodded and smiled as I told them about the sensation of being one with everything, but I couldn't be sure they understood what I meant. Deep inside I knew it really didn't matter if anyone could relate to that feeling of ecstasy, yet I wanted to share my new insight with everyone around me.

At 5:30 a.m. I left Tara's room with Katey to catch our flight back to San Francisco. On the plane, I attempted to study for my Geology test, but the pages kept dissolving into sparkles of light. I concentrated as long I could, and finally drifted off to sleep.

I arrived for my mid-term a little sleepy, yet intensely aware of every sound, color, and texture around me. The test was multiple-choice, and the answers seemed to pop off the page in front of me as I read through each question. I hardly thought during the test. Rather, it seemed I just knew most of the answers because my mind was so clear. When I was unsure of an answer, I closed my eyes until I could remember the lecture about that topic. In the silence of my mind, I transported myself back to that moment and found the answers I needed.

A feeling of weightlessness stayed with me for several weeks after the event. Meditation came easily: As soon as I sat down, my mind became very still, letting the ecstasy of light fill me. I felt like I was falling in love over and over. On my days off, I often sat in the rose garden in Golden Gate Park, just enjoying the bliss of life.

My months of searching for an apartment finally paid off in December, when I found a tiny one-bedroom near the beach. After seeing the garden through the kitchen window, I knew it was my home. The very next weekend, Matthew helped me move my things with his van. Once he left, I began sorting through the piles of stuff, happy to be unpacking in my own apartment at last.

INTO THE DESERT MOUNTAIN

In the desert,
there is all and there is nothing.
God is there and man is not.
-Balzac

To celebrate the Winter Solstice, Tara invited me and her other students to sit with Rama in the Southern Californian desert. Hundreds of students from seven cities across America caravanned to the outskirts of a gorge in 4-wheel drive vehicles to meet Rama in the stillness of the desert night.

I watched the shooting stars race across the sky while we anticipated his arrival. The moonlight spilled down onto the jagged branches of thin trees and glittered on the sand, making the desert seem like a scene from a fantasy novel. Everything was so quiet, as if the night had absorbed all sound. The only words spoken were in whispers, and even those were few and far between. Too mesmerized by the stars to talk, I stood alone, leaning against our rented Ford Explorer.

Rama arrived wearing a bright yellow ski suit

and a huge grin. In a heavy Mexican accent, he warned of the enchanted taco who roamed the desert looking for lost souls. As I watched from the edge of the circle we had formed around him, Rama's body took on the shape of a gnarled old Mexican. We all howled with laughter, until he suddenly switched to a more serious tone in both his voice and mannerisms.

"This is a place of power," he continued, standing straight and tall like a powerful sorcerer. "Do not ever come down here alone, especially at night. There are forces and energies out here that could destroy you. The desert has a way of drawing you in. The next ridge always looks closer than it is and everything looks the same for miles in every direction. All you have to do is make a couple of turns and you'll be completely confused. If you go wandering out here, it's very easy to get lost and there's no one out here to find you.

"We're going to drive deeper into the gorge now," he added, turning to face each of us in the circle. "Keep a respectful distance between you and the car in front of you because the sand is deep and people may get stuck, but don't lose sight of them."

We followed him down the bumpy roads that had been carved in the sand by past floods and previous 4-wheel drive trucks. The spiny trees seemed to close from behind, separating us from the world I knew. As we drove in silence, my mind slowly settled and my fears relaxed their grip. I felt safe with Rama in the desert, even though I could feel things out here that clearly were not physical.

Although I had been wearing shorts only a few hours earlier, I was now freezing under three layers of clothing. Shivering in the cold, I was thankful someone had told me about the rapid drop in temperature in the desert after sunset. Even bundled up under scarves, gloves and extra sweaters, I still felt I was slowly becoming a human popsicle.

We sat in a semi-circle, facing a stone ridge that loomed above us like a mountain covered with dark shadows. Rama strolled out to the center, looking taller than he had at the first meeting place. He continued his antics about the enchanted taco, bringing in his brother the burrito, and soon had everyone laughing hysterically.

Rama then walked around the circle and stood directly in front of each of us. As he stood before me, waves of heat radiated from his being. The cold melted from my face as my body relaxed.

"What you're feeling is called tumo. It's a siddha that many monks who live in the Himalayas learn out of necessity. This siddha allows you to warm your body by using kundalini, which is very useful if you're meditating in a cave in the Himalayas. You're a little warmer now, yeah?" he asked with a smile.

The group mumbled an agreement as he continued with a stern voice, "It's very cold in the Himalayas, colder than here, so stop complaining. We could be sitting in a cave up there with ten feet of snow and the wind whipping right through us. So this isn't so bad. Stop focusing on the cold and look over here," he commanded.

"The energy of this gorge is as close to Tibet as I have been able to find in the United States," he began again as he slowly moved towards the center of the circle. "Its vibration level is about the same. This place is an inter-dimensional vortex – from here you can move fairly easily into other dimensions."

I glanced at his feet as he crossed the sand. He didn't pick them up as you normally would when you walked. Instead, he was gliding across the sand on what appeared to be thin golden strands of energy or light. As I watched, his legs completely disappeared. He stretched his arms towards the sky, and they grew ten feet long. He reminded me of a cartoon, but I was too awestruck to laugh.

"Now look at the top of the ridge," he called out from what sounded to be far off in the distance.

The mountain began to glow with a soft golden hue, blocking out the light from the stars. Then I saw a figure, the same size and shape as Rama, bouncing along the top edge of the cliff. I looked back down to the sand, but I couldn't see Rama anywhere in the circle. Up on the ridge, I saw him clearly, dancing in the light.

I felt two parts of me struggling for control. On one side, this whole display of miracles seemed completely normal while the other part of my mind kept chattering on about the impossibility of these occurrences. No matter what I thought, however, I couldn't deny what I was seeing with my own eyes. I was sure I was about to go completely mad when he appeared again on the ground.

"Everything here is taking place in the second attention, so you've probably just seen some pretty incredible things," said Rama from the center of the circle, his body glowing with light. "It's good to talk about what you witnessed, just so you know that you didn't imagine it. So, let's hear some experiences." He looked at us expectantly.

"I saw you gliding across the sand on what looked like ropes, and then you would disappear at certain times," said a woman across from me.

"Those are the lines of the world," replied Rama in a clear, strong voice. "Where the lines come together are access points to other worlds. When I disappear, I go to the other dimensions and open them up for you. They pass through you, and if you have enough power, you can become aware of them.

"Everything is made of energy," he continued, his words resounding deep into the night. "The energy lines you see hold the dimensions together in a complex web of light. As you become more advanced in your knowledge of the occult worlds, you learn how the dimensions fit together. This knowledge can eventually help you to go beyond dimensionality into realms of pure light.

"But you don't need to worry about that now. Just by being here with me, you're being empowered. It takes lifetimes of practice to learn how to maintain the high states of awareness that you're in right now.

"Also, if you don't see anything, don't feel bad," added Rama. "It just means that your aura is blocked, and it will eventually clear if you keep meditating. You're still absorbing a lot of energy that you can use to improve your meditation.

"Now, focus on me as I become a doorway, and try to go into the mountain."

I used all of my will power to still my mind, and directed my attention towards Rama. Shafts of gold light sprang from his body, like ribbons from a Maypole. With my mind, I connected with one of the ribbons. Suddenly, I was flying through him and up to the mountain. I was facing a door, which I knew to be locked. Then a key appeared, and I slipped into the mountain. I didn't have a body, yet I was acutely aware of the power and solid strength of this place. Allowing myself to become completely absorbed by the mountain, the feeling of coming home after a long journey washed over me.

In the distance, I felt rather than heard Rama calling us back from the mountain. I didn't want to leave the sanctuary I had found there, but his call pulled me reluctantly back to my body. As I came back to the physical world, I was surrounded by a sense of tranquility I had not known since I was a small child.

"The desert to me is like going home," said Rama as we prepared to leave. "A part of me is always here, so when you think of this place, you'll find me."

As we drove into the violet and orange of the desert sunrise, I knew that I too had found a home in the desert.

OUT OF THE NEST

*The Pathway to Enlightenment
Is the one that gives Joy.*
                                        -Rama

After the desert trip, I flew to Boston to visit my family for Christmas. The last time I had seen my parents was the previous summer when they had come to visit me in San Francisco, before I met Rama.

We had talked on the phone during the past few months, but I had cut most of our conversations short, simply because they never seemed to have anything positive to talk about. My mother would complain about her work, and my father would grumble about my brothers, who were still struggling to make their way in the world.

Meditation had sparked my excitement about life, and although my part time jobs didn't pay very much, they were fun and flexible with the time I had to work. I was too happy to worry about how hard life could be. There was too much fun to be had, and not enough time to focus on the negative aspects of life.

At my parents' house, I talked to my mother about how she could improve her resume and try for a better job. She was working as a computer programmer, and from what I had heard at the seminars, she could earn a much higher rate than she thought. She didn't believe me, and told me my friends must be wrong. I couldn't defend what I knew, since my knowledge was based on what Rama and my friends had told me, rather than my own experience.

Each night at my parents' house, I went home relatively early to meditate and sleep. It was great to catch up with my old friends, but I was bored with getting drunk and talking about the past. Early every morning, I went jogging in the frozen air and meditated in the woods down the street.

On the morning I was to fly back to San Francisco, I woke up on the couch while my mother was making breakfast. She noticed I was awake, so she came into the living room to give me a hug.

"What's going on with you? You've changed so much," she asked with concern.

"You know that I started meditating, Mom. It makes a difference. Anyway, all the changes are for the good, right? I'm happier, I dress better, and I'm doing better in school. Why are you worried?"

"I know," she conceded. "It's just strange, that's all. You're not like you used to be and that makes me nervous."

"Oh, would you rather have me out getting drunk every night like I used to? Personally, I think that would be kind of boring," I retorted.

"No, you're right. Just don't stop calling, and try to visit more often." The fine lines of age and worry creased her blue eyes. I knew she meant well, but her unasked questions about Rama made me defensive.

As the plane left the ground that day, I sighed with relief. I had enjoyed seeing everyone, but it was obvious that no one there was interested in meditation or self-discovery. I wanted to share what I was learning with my family and friends, but even my mother was suspicious of Rama. They just didn't get it. Whenever the subject had been brought up, a battle began because I felt I had to defend my beliefs, and it was just too draining for me. There was no way they would believe I had meditated in a room with a man who turned the place gold.

In San Francisco, I continued to meditate and run on the beach every day. My little apartment started to feel more like home as I put things in order and hung pictures on the wall. Within a few days, I had recovered from the visit to my parents' house and put my disappointment that they couldn't appreciate my study of meditation behind me.

The month of January flew by as I processed the miracles I had seen in the desert and the disbelief of my friends and family. When spring semester began, I didn't have the time to wonder why I couldn't talk about Rama to my parents and my old friends. I poured all of my attention into my school work, breaking the monotony by writing poems in my notebook between classes.

After a late night at class, I wound my way

along the walkway with a smile curled on my lips, feeling so incredibly alive and energized I could have danced till dawn. Like a picture on a postcard, the full moon hung low in the indigo sky, shimmering on the dew the fog had left on the grass. I suddenly realized I should have been completely exhausted. I had been averaging about four hours sleep each night between my two jobs, full-time classes, and meditating for an hour in both the morning and evening. On top of my already insane schedule, I had also joined a karate class that met twice a week.

I remembered how cold last winter had seemed, and laughed to myself thinking back to how miserable I had been. *So this is what it feels like to study with an Enlightened teacher*, I realized as I crossed the street to catch the bus home.

Tara had called me the previous week to tell me she would no longer be my mentor because Rama had officially accepted me as his student. She also mentioned that he had plans for her and the other intermediate students to work on a project in Chicago. I had only known her for a few months, but I knew I would miss her.

She told me, "It's a happy thing – we're all moving forward. You've just graduated from Buddhist kindergarten! Just remember all Rama wants is for you to be yourself; do that and you'll be fine."

On Saturday, Katey drove Anthony, Tanya, Matthew, and me up through the fog on Mount Tamalpais to the amphitheater. It was the first time we were allowed to see Rama without having Tara as our guide. Matthew and Katey talked about Tara the entire ride, exchanging stories about the adventures they had shared with her. Anthony, Tanya, and I listened from the back seat as they shared their memories with each other. Secretly I wondered why they were so nervous without Tara. She had been a wonderful mentor, but from the first time I meditated with Rama, I knew he was my teacher, not her.

The brisk February air made me dig my hands into my pockets as I sat down on one of the wooden benches where everyone had gathered. As soon as Rama arrived, I completely forgot about the cold.

"Hi!" exclaimed Rama from the ground in front of us. "Nice day, huh?"

I smiled and nodded in agreement, noting that the other students around me were doing the same. Rama always seemed so happy – his excitement about life reminded me of a child ripping open birthday presents.

"Well, here we are," said Rama, looking around at the crowd gathered before him. "What can I do for you today?"

"Why aren't there more Enlightened women?" asked a young Asian woman from the left side of the amphitheater.

"Good question," he answered with a smile.

"It has to do with energy, power, and tradition," continued Rama in a light, casual tone. "Anyone can attain Enlightenment, but it takes energy to reach beyond ordinary experience and into Enlightened states of consciousness. This energy is called kundalini, and it sits dormant in the base of the spine until it is either consciously activated through meditation, or until the body needs it for some reason like creating a child or in a survival situation.

"Women naturally have more energy than men because they need it to bear children, but men on the other hand, have the power in society. That's just the way society has evolved. Many traditional Buddhist sects don't believe women can attain Enlightenment. They say that women are not as evolved as men and that they must be reborn as a man in order to become Enlightened. If this were a traditional Buddhist monastery in the Far East, women would not be allowed in the room with an Enlightened master. In an exceptional case, the nuns may possibly be allowed to sit in the back, but they certainly would not be able to ask questions like you.

"Enlightenment doesn't care what sex you are, but you do need to meditate," continued Rama. "So, if you can't find a master to teach you the advanced meditation techniques, you won't be able to pull up enough energy to move beyond the self."

Rama paused for a moment, as if to give us time to absorb what he was saying.

"We all have a luminous shell composed of fibers of energy that surrounds our bodies, which is sometimes referred to as the aura or subtle body. When a woman has a baby, her energy is used to create the luminous fibers of the child. That energy is gone from the woman, so she cannot use it to reach higher states of consciousness. Birth literally leaves a hole in the subtle body, which is a constant drain for the woman. Even though she is no longer carrying the child in her physical body, they are still connected on an energy level."

My body tensed as he spoke. Something within

me did not want to hear that I had to choose between children and the search for Enlightenment. I was only twenty-two years old, and I certainly wasn't ready to make that kind of decision. I had never really wanted to have a baby, but the idea of not being able to if I wanted to practice meditation made me angry; it just didn't seem fair.

"A mother can still benefit from meditation," added Rama, as if he had heard my thoughts. "But you have to understand that it is much more difficult for her to reach higher states of awareness than it would be if she didn't have a child. And of course, there are very complex techniques through which she may be able to attain Enlightenment, but she would have to already be very advanced on the path."

"Rama, is it better to be celibate?" asked a young man hesitantly after Rama had acknowledged his raised hand with a nod.

"It's not better or worse," replied Rama patiently. "You have to decide what works for you. I teach meditation and Buddhist yoga, but I don't tell people how to live. What you do with your life is entirely up to you. I often make suggestions, but what I say to one person may not work for another, so it's really your decision of how you want to live.

"Some people need to have that kind of relationship. It gives them some sense of stability. If they're not in a relationship, they spend all of their energy looking for one and they can't advance with meditation or in their careers. For other people, a relationship isn't worth the investment. They would rather put their time and energy into other things that make them happy.

"Try to understand, though, that your body wants to make a baby; it's coded into your genes. Your body uses kundalini to create a new life by pulling the energy through the sex organs when you have an orgasm. It doesn't matter whether or not a baby is created, that energy is still released.

"Think of kundalini like the energy in a battery – you only have so much. If you use it during sex, there isn't much kundalini left for meditation or other things that you may enjoy. This is well known by professional athletes. They won't have sex right before a competition because sex burns up energy.

"Again, that's not good or bad," continued Rama. "You have to decide how you're going to use your energy. Occultists use kundalini to change their level of awareness and go to different worlds. But maybe that's not right for you. Maybe it's enough just to meditate and put your energy into a family or whatever else makes you happy. That's for you to figure out."

While listening to him talk, the wind started to blow, moving the fog up from the base of the mountain. A soft gold light around Rama's body grew steadily brighter, and I had to pinch myself to be sure I wasn't dreaming. My earlier frustration faded away as I watched the light radiate from his being. Even though I had seen the golden glow around Rama before, it was still a mystery to me.

"Please understand," said Rama. "Buddhism is an inner study; it's a very private thing. A teacher can guide you along the path, and make corrections, but it's up to you to find what brings you up to higher states of consciousness. There are many pathways to Enlightenment, and the one I teach is not right for everyone." He looked at the man who had asked the question with compassion, as if to say he understood the confusion the man was feeling.

"I've read all of your applications, which means that I've looked at each of you psychically. You could say that I've read between the lines of what you wrote." As he spoke, Rama moved his gaze over the crowd. "It's really interesting how many similarities I noticed. Not just here in the Bay area, but across all seven cities where I've been teaching, many of you have had the same experiences.

"One thing that stood out was that you're all survivors. There were a surprisingly large number of people who have been sexually abused or have been addicted to drugs and alcohol. In deference to the reformed alcoholics, I won't be serving alcohol at any of our events. I don't want those who don't drink to feel like they should because I have it available at the events. There's nothing wrong with drinking, but some people use it to escape from the pain they feel from living in the world. It's crucial that you learn to deal with the pain if you want to continue on a spiritual path as intense as Tantric Buddhism. It's easy to drown yourself in alcohol and drugs, but it takes a warrior to be able to carry on without a crutch."

The sun began to set, sending pink and orange streaks through the fog. As the sky overhead dimmed to a deep violet, Rama let us know that it was time to go home.

"Before you leave, let me make a couple of announcements. On April 1, there will be an ordination in New York that you're all invited to attend. If you can't afford to go to the East coast, don't worry because there will be another ordination. I'll give you more details when we meet next month.

"Have a great night, and I'll see you in March."

Completely elated, Anthony, Tanya, Matthew, Katey, and I drove down the mountain back to San Francisco. Not one of us spoke about the trip to New York. I knew I wanted to go, but my bank account was nearly empty and getting time off from work would be next to impossible. Instead, I pushed my worries about the trip out of my mind and simply enjoyed the ride home.

A few days later at the bank where I worked, I stood staring at the calendar. My boss walked by and I instinctively stopped her to say I was taking a few days off at the beginning of April. She looked over the calendar, said it was all right, and walked away. Stunned, I continued on my way out for lunch.

"Tanya," I said from the phone in the break room. "My boss just gave me the Friday and Saturday off in April for the ordination. I didn't even know I was asking for it off until it came out of my mouth."

"Wow! That's great," she replied. "Yesterday I saw an ad for group airline rates to New York. We just need to get thirty people to sign up and we can get round-trip tickets for $250."

"No way! That is so cool," I exclaimed. "I'm sure we can get at least that many together. Matthew has a bunch of phone numbers of people in the study. I'll call him tonight."

"Great! Tell him to call me after you talk to him," said Tanya. "I'm going to try to get a group rate at the hotel too. Someone told me the Greenwich Hyatt is nice."

"Definitely. I can't believe I'm actually going. But you know, the more I think about it, I wouldn't miss this for the world," I said before hanging up.

The next few weeks flew by as we made plans for the pilgrimage to New York. In March, all of the new students went to the movies with Rama to see *Groundhog Day*. In the lobby after the movie, Tanya was surrounded by a small group of students discussing the trip. While I waited for her to finish, Rama walked up and stood next to me. I looked around nervously at the woman's backpack in front of me, and realized I had to either turn my back towards Rama to join the group or start a conversation with him.

"Tanya's organizing the New York trip so we can get a group fare," I said to him, explaining why we were still in the lobby of the theater.

"That's outstanding!" replied Rama, looking at me intently.

Awe-struck, I smiled and searched for something intelligent to say.

"New York's a tough place," he said, ignoring my uneasiness. "The energy can be very intense. The best way to deal with it is to exercise. Do push-ups."

"Yeah, I've been running on the beach and it's great," I answered, confident that I had been doing plenty of exercise.

"That's good. But do push-ups." Rama looked up as the group around Tanya began to break up. With a smile, he stepped back and patiently waited for us to clear out of the lobby.

THE BATTLE BEGINS

That which does not kill me
Makes me stronger.
                    -Nietzsche

I woke on Sunday to the city submerged in fog. Determined to find some sun, I journeyed to the Mission district, which was protected from fog by Twin Peaks. On my way out of a small bookstore, I ran into Anthony.

"Hey, what's going on?" he asked as we met on the sidewalk. His short blond hair was a bit ruffled from the wind, but he had one of those faces that looked good with messy hair.

"Oh nothing, just hanging out in the sun. The Richmond is total fog city. Have you eaten? I'm dying for crepes – every time I'm down here, I have to have them."

We walked to my favorite crepe place on 16th Street near the Roxie theater, dodging a small group of drunks leaving the local bar.

"So where have you been? I haven't seen you around for a while," I asked as we sat down with our food at the table near the window.

"I started computer school a few weeks ago, so I've been programming away. And I also went to visit my parents in Southern California."

"You're going to computer school too? It seems like all of Rama's students are into computers. I just can't picture myself working on one all day," I said before taking a bite of cheese and mushroom filled crepe.

"Computers are great! I don't know why, but I love it," said Anthony. "The feeling you get from seeing a program you wrote work is incredible. It's like magic."

"How are your parents doing?" I asked, changing the subject.

"They're, well," he continued with hesitation, "a bit confused. Basically, they set me up. I knew I shouldn't have gone down there, but my mom really wanted to see me, so I went."

"What do you mean, they set you up?" I asked.

"When I walked into the house, there were four people talking to my parents that I had never seen before. We all sat down in the living room together, and they started asking me tons of questions about Rama and the study. They had my parents completely freaked out, telling them Rama was brainwashing a bunch of people in San Francisco," replied Anthony, shaking his head.

"Wow! I can't believe your parents let them in the house." I wondered if they were from the same group Matthew had warned me about last fall.

"Neither could I, but these people had my parents convinced. I noticed this one guy seemed to be controlling the meeting, so I told him to talk to me outside. We went out to the front yard and he tried to talk me into joining Cult Watch and spying on Rama's seminars. He said he had been one of Rama's students, and he knew that Rama was a fake. When I refused, he started telling me how powerful he was and that he could teach me all about magic and how to levitate and stuff."

"Was he for real?" I asked, shocked that the Cult Watch people were able to find out he was a student and where his parents lived.

"I doubt it. He was a serious power-monger, though. I laughed at him at first, and then he started getting nasty and threatening me, so I kicked him off the property. Once he left, the others joined him without a word. Fortunately, my parents listened to me. I think my being in computer school helped them realize that Rama's seminars are helping me more than hurting."

"I still can't believe anyone would actually do that," I said.

"My folks told me they wanted $10,000 to kidnap me from San Francisco, and that for an extra fee, they would have me 'deprogrammed' from Rama's teachings."

"Wow, that is really scary. I'm kind of glad my parents don't have a lot of money. I don't know what they would do if someone showed up at their door with the same story. I saw my folks over Christmas, and my mom was a bit freaked out. I guess she didn't expect me to actually start talking about doing something with my life. If someone showed up at their door and told them I was being brainwashed, I don't know what they would do."

"Some parents must be willing to pay them, or

else there wouldn't be people out there making money from it," said Anthony. "I guess some people don't have anything better to do than try to control other people's lives."

The next day the sun burned through the fog, so I walked to the waterfall in Golden Gate Park to do my sociology homework, which was to read *The Communist Manifesto*. I climbed up to the ledge, where I often sat to write poetry and watch the birds play on the lake. The introduction dragged on, causing my eyes to close more than once. I drifted off and had a dream that Rama was sitting with me next to the waterfall, but he was levitating in the air above the water rather than sitting on the rocks. I woke with a start as I began to fall over in my sleep. I watched the water splashing against the rocks and realized this was definitely not a safe place to take a nap.

I gave up reading and went for a walk through the rose garden, thinking about Anthony's recent experience with the anti-cult people. When Matthew had first told me about Cult Watch, I didn't take him very seriously. Now that one of my friends had to deal with it face to face at his parents' house, I realized angry people can do some serious damage if they're the least bit coordinated. I couldn't understand why they went after Anthony, but it really didn't matter to me at that point.

The whole idea of people battling Rama in the physical world as well as on the astral plane was beyond me. Every time I had gone to his seminars, I had left feeling so elated that I couldn't imagine anyone wanting to hurt him. It just didn't make sense to try to destroy someone who brings so much joy into the world.

As for myself, I didn't worry about being kidnapped, since my parents didn't have very much money and they lived on the other side of the country. Nonetheless, I knew I wouldn't tell them I was about to be ordained as a Buddhist monk in New York.

APRIL ENCHANTMENT

Everything you contact
Is a place to practice the Way.
                    -the Obaku abbot Zuiun

On the evening of the ordination, silk thangkas depicting various deities and Enlightened beings of the Vajrayana tradition decorated the hall with the subtle elegance found in many oriental monasteries. The candles surrounding the bouquets of flowers on each table and the soft overhead lights added to the beauty, giving the room a magical feeling. As I observed the people and the room, I had the sensation of being in the ancient castle of some forgotten fairy tale.

"As my student," began Rama as he placed his ring and watch on the small black table next to his chair on stage. "you are constantly in my aura. When an Enlightened teacher accepts a student, an energy line is formed, and the student is constantly being empowered by the teacher. So you're actually getting energy from me all of the time, not just when you come to see me at a seminar.

"This is important for you to realize, because people will notice that you're different. They'll sense this energy from you and may get upset because they don't have it and they don't know how to get it. People get jealous very easily, so it's a good idea to be very low key about your life. They won't understand why you're so happy all of the time when they aren't."

As he spoke, I remembered the reaction from my family when I had seen them over Christmas. I began to realize they couldn't grasp why I was so happy when they were so miserable, and their jealousy had caused them to attack my beliefs.

"Here in the West, there isn't a reference point for Enlightenment, or a place for Buddhist monks, so even if you did try to explain it to them, they probably wouldn't get it. There are a few monasteries here in the States, but people in general don't really understand Eastern spiritual practice. Something you need to realize is you have a direct connection to the light of Enlightenment available to you at all times, and not many people, especially in the West, have that opportunity. Not because it isn't available, mind you, but because they can't comprehend that the light is there all the time. You, on the other hand, have seen it every time you've been to a seminar.

"I do have to tell you though," continued Rama, a smile curling on his lips, "this is quite interesting for me to have you as my students. To tell you the truth, I wasn't planning on accepting any new students for at least a few years. I wanted my intermediate students to teach you the basics, but things change fast around here and I have another project for them to work on. So that leaves me with you."

He looked around the room as if he were scanning the area for some sign of life. No one moved a muscle. As his gaze crossed the room, a gold light radiated from him, filling the hall.

"No, really, this is weird," he said playfully. "I don't know any of you at all, so I have no idea what to do with you. I've begun designing a program for you to work with me, but I don't know where it's going to take us.

"Basically, I teach by using projects to critique your awareness field. Most of what happens goes on in the second attention, so it's very difficult to get meaningful feedback from me without something concrete to look at. The major tool I use to teach is career. Now, you're not required to follow my suggestions, but if you want to work with me on a more practical level, we need something to talk about.

"Let me start by telling you about computer science," he continued, reminding me of a salesman. "Computer science is the most rapidly expanding field today, so it won't be a problem finding a job as long as you're qualified. It's also very good for women. Since it's so new, it hasn't become entirely male-dominated. Of course, there are mostly men in the field because men are usually encouraged to go into the hard sciences, but the need for good programmers is so great it really doesn't matter what sex you are. You can advance very rapidly in the computer science field, because it's one of the few places where they pay you based on your knowledge rather than time put into a company. So, you can quickly make a lot of money and never have a problem getting a job.

"But that's only part of the reason I suggest you go into computer science. In Tantric Buddhism, everything we do is our yoga. In other words, there is no separation from what is spiritual practice and what is not. In traditional Tibetan practice, the monks would memorize complex mandalas and meditate by holding these images in their minds until they could do it perfectly. Computer science forces you to do this as well. Only instead of mandalas, you hold different relational concepts in your mind as you work on a program or develop a system. The intensity of focus required to do the job right is so great that it's very similar to meditation. So you could think of it as getting paid to do Buddhist exercises all day.

"It's still important to do a good morning and evening meditation, though," explained Rama. As I watched him, his face began to change: his hair grew long and dark, and his jaw line became more oval. I kept blinking my eyes, but the Japanese man Rama had become on stage remained. "The silent meditation gives you the energy to stay focused all day, and by keeping your attention locked on to something like programming, you can remain in a high state of awareness. Then in the evening when you sit in meditation, it washes away any incorrect ideas you may have picked up during the day so you can have a nice night.

"This is the Enlightenment cycle. It's a process whereby every day, every month, every year you reach higher states of awareness. Enlightenment doesn't occur overnight; it takes lifetimes of dedicated practice. But some people like to go faster, so they take the short path. By using every moment to direct your consciousness towards Enlightenment, you can speed up the process," concluded Rama.

He then gave us instructions to stand before him, one at a time. He said he would touch our third eye, and then we could sit back down and meditate while everyone took a turn. Since I was at the front table, I was one of the first to be ordained, or "put on the path" as Rama called it.

As I meditated, I became aware of a sharp pain in my lower back. I tried to adjust my position and ignore the pain, but it continued to grow. I thought about leaving the room to stretch and walk around a bit, but I knew that would be completely inappropriate. I didn't want to appear rude, especially in front of my teacher, so I gritted my teeth and focused with greater determination on the music playing in the background.

When I could not concentrate any longer, and the pain was literally searing my back, I opened my eyes to look at Rama. Everyone was seated, and he was meditating in the lotus position on stage. In his face, I saw an expression of sheer agony. I realized the pain I was feeling was nothing compared to the energy he had just taken through his body by touching each one of us. I understood without being told that he was literally taking all of our pain and healing our psychic scars with the light that came through him.

I watched with renewed respect as he went through what appeared to be a private battle. I wanted to help ease his pain, but I didn't know what to do. Within minutes, his face softened and he smiled as if he had won the battle. I kept focusing on the light that was flowing from him, and suddenly I felt my heart chakra burst open. I had the sensation of flying through the air, and I passed into his being. Everything stopped and I no longer felt my body. The only thing I was aware of was a warm golden light that enveloped me like sunshine on a mid-summer day.

When I returned to my body, my back pain had ceased completely. My mind was so clear I didn't need to think about anything. My private worries about my direction in life vanished. I knew in my heart everything would work out and I would know what to do when I needed to do it.

During the break I told the woman sitting next to me about my experiences. She listened with interest and then told me about the gold light she had seen while meditating. We were both amazed by the miracles we had seen since we had begun studying with Rama.

Once we were all seated again, Rama started off the second half by telling us about some of the projects his intermediate students were working on. One of them, who owned her own company, had made over two million dollars last year with her project and was expected to make ten million this year. I found out later he had been talking about Tara.

"Don't let the money thing bother you," he continued. "A lot of people think if you're spiritual, you have to be poor. That is the most ridiculous thing I've ever heard. Sure, maybe in the days when you could go live in a monastery and grow your own food and not have to deal with the world, you could live without owning anything.

"But you have to accept the fact that you do live in the world, and since you are spiritually inclined, you feel things more intensely than most people, which means you're going to have to pay to find a decent place where you can meditate. As most of you have probably already discovered, your meditations are much more powerful when you are in a nicer environment. That's why we hold our seminars in expensive hotels. It feels better; it's not as psychically polluted, so it's easier to reach higher levels. That's not to say that if you can't afford to live in a nice neighborhood right now you can't meditate. All I'm saying is you can insulate yourself by putting your body in a less abrasive place," explained Rama.

"If your environment is dragging you down all day and you have to fight to stay in a high state of mind, you won't have any energy to meditate. And then you'll be dragged down even further each day that you don't meditate. It's the same concept as going higher each day that you do meditate, only backwards. So get over the money thing. Everybody needs money to live in the world, and just because you meditate you're not an exception to the rule. Other rules, yes. For example, you don't have to put up with a dreary existence. Instead you can live in worlds of power and light by meditating.

"So this leads me to your first assignment. See, now that you're all monks, I get to give you work," said Rama with a mischievous grin. "The first assignment is to be happy at the end of each day. And the second is to achieve material success. It could be worse, you know," he continued as he looked at the faces in the audience. "I could tell you have to attain Enlightenment, and now that you're monks, it means you have to do it."

Immediately, my rebellious self jumped to attention. Anything someone told me I *had* to do automatically became something I would refuse to do. I pushed the thought out of my head; after all, they were really good assignments. Who could complain about being happy and successful?

Sensing many of us cringing at the idea of being told what to do, Rama continued to point out that we had agreed to be his students by becoming monks. "I'm serious. The assignments I give you need to be done, but it is your karma, so you can do whatever you want. Just remember, it will follow you. Being a monk is something you should take very seriously, but don't forget your first assignment: be happy at the end of each day. And, of course, you need to be materially successful. I've already explained why, so don't whine about it."

Some people, myself included, were obviously worried about being required to be materially successful. The idealist in me was convinced I could do what Rama asked, but the rational side of my brain cringed at the thought of even trying. Rama teased us by making jokes about the looks on some of the students' faces when he had mentioned being successful.

I hated the games people who have money play, acting as if they owned the world. Most of my friends were poor, and I had already accepted it as my fate. As a bank teller I understood all too well the attitude of being better than others that rich people often displayed. Rama and the intermediate students, however, never exhibited that attitude at any of the seminars, so perhaps it wasn't the money itself that caused it, I reasoned. For the first time in my life, I allowed myself to toy with the idea of being wealthy.

On the plane ride home to San Francisco, I fell asleep with my head on Matthew's shoulder. He had moved to San Jose after graduating from computer school to be close to his new job, so the ordination was the first time I had seen him outside of a seminar in several months. When I woke up as the plane began its descent, I was a bit embarrassed, but Matthew just smiled without saying a word.

A few weeks later, Matthew invited me to go hiking in Marin County. We followed a trail that had not been used for quite some time. Bright green brush crowded the path in some places and the fallen branches from the redwoods had not been cleared since the winter storms. Matthew explained that when he was younger, he would always hike out here because not too many people knew about it.

As we talked and laughed I felt as if I had known Matthew my entire life. Our hands collided as we walked, and Matthew gently grabbed hold of my fingers. The trail eventually lead to a pond, where we planned to eat lunch before heading back.

The sun blazed overhead, and although it was only May, we were both roasting from the hike. We decided to go skinny-dipping to cool off, and soon found ourselves in each other's arms. Lunch was forgotten until the sun began sinking in the western trees.

"We should start back, or else we'll end up walking in the dark," said Matthew, looking up at the sky.

"It's a beautiful sunset," I replied, watching the red sun dip closer to the treetops. "But, you're right. I would hate to get lost out here."

"You know, I haven't made love in over five years," confessed Matthew as he put on his clothes. "There was a time when I slept with a different girl every week, but when I started looking into spirituality sex kind of lost its appeal. And after I went to India, I just decided to be celibate."

"What a wonderful place to break your celibacy," I answered, caught off guard by his disclosure. "So does that mean you don't want this to happen again?"

"No, no." he answered, taking my hand in his as we walked down the path. "It was great, and I'd love to do it again. But honestly, I want to keep it discrete. I really don't want to be thought of as a couple at the seminars. I go there to see Rama, and I don't want to be distracted from that."

"That's reasonable," I agreed. "I would hate to be the subject of the current gossip; I hear enough of it as it is. There's no way I want to be the topic of discussion, especially at one of the events." I looked at him with a smile, feeling like a school girl with a secret to keep from her best friends.

During the next few weeks Matthew drove up to teach me different computer programs on his laptop computer and to hear me read poetry at Sacred Grounds coffee shop. I had attended only a few open readings, and his presence made me more comfortable reading love poems in public.

At first, I resisted learning anything about Windows or the other software programs he wanted to teach me. By the second or third time I had used the mouse and played on the computer, however, I felt more confident and began to look forward to learning more about the technology.

When Matthew noticed I had started reading the magazines he left for me instead of throwing them away, he gave me an old 286 desktop computer a friend of his didn't need anymore. A few weeks passed before I sat down to figure out how to make my diskette with Word Perfect for DOS run on the outdated machine so I could type some poems to enter in a poetry contest.

Katey and Tanya quickly put together why Matthew was spending so much time in San Francisco. I pretended my interest was purely in learning computers and talking about meditation, but I was sure they knew the truth.

Matthew embraced everything Rama said at the seminars with enthusiasm, always eager to try out the latest technique or idea in the real world. His first job as a programmer earning $30,000 a year convinced me a computer career might not be a bad idea. His devotion to Rama bordered on fanaticism, but I had to admit Rama's suggestions worked, and Matthew was living proof.

Matthew thanked Rama in part by taking care of the stage furniture he used at the seminars. After setting up the furniture at the hotel, Matthew would come to my house to shower and dress for the banquet. We shared passionate kisses while I waited for Katey to pick me up, and promised not to look at each other during the seminar. Some nights, especially during the breaks, I couldn't wait to meet Matthew afterwards for another evening of lovemaking.

Katey and Anthony were both well on their way to becoming computer professionals by earning a certificate in computer programming, and I had never seen Tanya happier to be alive. Although we were all having fun, each of us had our own battles to fight. The students attending Computer Learning Center had to explain to the teacher why half the class was absent every time Rama gave a seminar, without giving the school administration reason to worry about a harmful cult invading their school. Tanya was struggling to balance her finances; however, whenever she needed money to see Rama, she would always find a way. And I was falling in love with Matthew.

On the way home from a seminar, Katey asked me straight out if I was having an affair with Matthew. I knew immediately she had seen Matthew's van parked on my street when she picked me up. Since Tara had left, Katey and I had grown apart, and I didn't feel like my relationship with Matthew was any of her business, but she insisted on knowing. There was no sense in lying to her, so I admitted we had been seeing each other, but refused to go into detail when she asked. After that confrontation, I decided it was time to buy my own car.

The next day, after Matthew left, I re-examined my talk with Katey. Why was I so defensive? I realized it was because I was getting in over my head emotionally, and there was nothing she could do to help me sort it out. With a sigh, I indulged in thoughts about creating a home with Matthew.

STEPPING THROUGH THE NIGHT

A shooting star falls in the East,
Altering the ancient lights
That stretch across the sky,
Mirroring diamonds in the sand

In June, Rama invited us to the desert with him for the Summer Solstice. For many of the new students, this was their first desert trip with Rama. Twilight gave way to the night stars as we waited on the sand, most of us sitting on the hoods of our Jeeps. I couldn't even look at Matthew because I knew my face would betray my feelings for him. We had shared the rented Grand Cherokee with Anthony, Katey, and Tanya, so I wandered away from the group before anyone noticed.

When Rama arrived, we followed him deep into the desert, our Jeeps churning up dust clouds of dry sand, slowing our progress. I sat in the back, next to Katey, watching the Jeeps rocking and bouncing as we passed into the gorge and into the second attention.

We seated ourselves as quickly as possible

around the base of a ridge. Even though there were nearly four hundred of us present, I still felt as if I were attending an intimate gathering. Compared to the immensity of the desert around us and the stars above, our party was a tiny speck of dust. As I looked up at the mountain before me, I forgot all about my desire to be with Matthew.

"Since there are so many of you, there may be times when you can't hear or see me," yelled Rama across the wide expanse of people. "I'll keep moving from end to end, but no matter where you're sitting, you'll still absorb the energy."

My head began to tingle as flickers of gold light emanated from Rama. His legs grew very long, and he became extremely tall, like the twenty-foot Indian I had seen the first time I meditated with Tara in Marin. As he walked around, Rama climbed an invisible staircase that led to another world where I couldn't see him. Then his feet would also disappear, leaving only his knees visible.

"Watch the top of the ridge," he yelled from the other end of the circle, his voice strong yet very distant.

A small party of Indian warriors looked down at us from the cliff. Rama began a slow, rhythmic chant as he walked around the circle clapping his hands. In the distance, I heard the warriors chanting along with the music of a rattle and drum. My mind kept screaming that this was impossible, but I knew on a deeper level it was all very real. When I let myself think about what was happening, the chanting would stop and I would see only a group of people sitting under the stars. The rattle, however, would continue to shake as I tried to think of a rational explanation. Eventually, I convinced myself that it was only a discarded can blowing around in the wind.

"What did you see?" asked Rama a few minutes after he stopped clapping. "It's helpful to talk about your experiences because it solidifies them in your mind. It's pretty wild stuff, huh?"

A murmur of agreement passed through the crowd.

"I saw a bunch of beings on the rocks up there," said one woman in a hesitant voice.

"Those are warrior beings from another dimension that parallels this one. They thought it was funny that I brought you guys out to a place this powerful," laughed Rama.

"I heard a rattle," called out a man from the other end of the circle.

"Yeah!" exclaimed Rama. "Isn't that cool?" His excitement was contagious. I found myself watching the swirl of color surrounding Rama with a smile plastered to my face despite my earlier doubts.

"Rama?" inquired a woman's voice from behind me.

"That's me!" he answered in a perky tone.

"I saw you disappear, almost completely a few times. Then I would see you in another part of the circle."

"I need to work on the knees, right?"

"Yes!" she laughed as the rest of us giggled.

"When you can't see me, I'm stepping through to other dimensions," he explained. "This place is an inter-dimensional vortex, where many different worlds meet. By coming out here with your teacher, you can experience those other worlds, if you make yourself available to power by meditating."

"Rama, what do you mean by power?" asked a young man quietly.

"What?" said Rama. "I can hardly hear you."

"Could you explain what you mean by power?" he said louder, sounding irritated at having to raise his voice.

"Power, in its most basic definition, is the ability to perceive," began Rama. "There are an infinite amount of dimensions, or bands of perception, and depending on how open you are, how much power you have, you can experience different levels of awareness. Power is what holds the dimensions together, and by accessing a dimension, you access the power of that dimension.

"When we say a place is powerful, it means the energy of the place vibrates very quickly and if you can tune into that energy, you can see things very clearly. Notice how your attention is sharp and everything looks very crisp and bright right now. That's because this is a place of power, and by focusing on me, you change your awareness level to the dimensions I hold open for you.

"If you came here alone you might, if you didn't know what you were doing, attune yourself to some of the lower dimensions that are here as well. The lower dimensions will actually drain your energy because they vibrate slower, and you won't feel as good. So don't try it. It's not a good idea."

Rama glowed as he stood in front of the man who had asked the question. By the cold, hard look on his face, it seemed Rama had read more into the question than I had. Strength emanated from Rama as the young man cowered before him, suddenly humbled.

"This isn't a game," continued Rama. "When you step into the occult, everything you do matters. Right now, you're becoming empowered with an incredible amount of energy, and what you do with it is up to you. You could become completely egotistical and think you can control people, or you could do something really beautiful. Just remember, every thought and every action has an extra force behind it now that you study with me. You could really hurt someone if you don't watch it."

The silence of the desert enveloped me as I breathlessly watched Rama walk to the center of the circle. The power and strength Rama embodied frightened me. His stance reminded me of the pictures of the wrathful deities of the Tantric tradition I had seen on my visit to the Asian art museum. A growing respect for Rama bloomed within me as I recognized the control over the power he possessed during his interaction with the young man's improper attitude. Up until that point, my image of Rama had been based entirely on his compassionate nature as a teacher of Buddhism – now I knew there was much more to him than what showed on the surface.

"Focus on the wind," said Rama, raising his hands towards the star-speckled sky. "The wind, just like the rain, can clean your aura. Dive into it, and let the wind carry you away."

A cool breeze danced with my hair, pulling it away from my face. My body felt lighter and lighter, until I could no longer feel anything physically. All I knew was the wind and the ecstatic sensation of flying.

As we left the desert, I thought about my life and the time I had wasted feeling trapped with no direction. Nothing I had ever accomplished, nothing I had ever seen, could compare with the limitless possibilities Rama revealed to me. I didn't really understand where it was I wanted to get to. All I knew was that wherever these worlds of power and worlds of light were, I wanted to go, no matter what the price.

THE JOURNEY EAST

Contemplate all energies
Without fear or disgust;
Find their essence,
For that is the stone
That turns everything to gold.
-Milarepa

Shortly after the desert trip, Rama announced he was moving the study to New York in October. He wanted to work with his new students all in one place, and New York provided the best opportunities for us. He also explained he would be offering computer seminars taught by his intermediate students in order to help us with our careers in the computer industry.

The news disturbed me; I couldn't possibly leave the Bay Area. San Francisco was the first place I lived where I truly felt at home. With the used car I had bought, I was just starting to explore some of the city's hidden corners. I struggled for weeks with the decision of whether or not to follow Rama. In my heart, I knew I would eventually have to go, but

I wanted to put it off as long as possible.

Matthew told me he was planning on moving to New York in September, which influenced my decision of when to move. Our love affair had become an important part of my life and I wanted it to continue on the east coast. After going to a party with some friends from the study, I had a dream of showing my new apartment in New York to Matthew and Anthony. The next morning I told Matthew about the dream, and that I had decided to leave San Francisco after the last seminar in mid-September.

Soon after, Matthew stopped attending the poetry readings and would not return my phone calls. I didn't hear from him for nearly a month, so I mailed him a poem to tell him I missed him. I cried all the pain away, and I didn't really expect him to answer my letter any more than he did my phone calls.

He caught me off guard when he came to visit shortly after reading the poem. I wanted to think that maybe there could be something between us, but his cold, distant eyes told me it was over. I laid out on the table how I felt, and that I was disappointed he chose to ignore me rather than talk to me about his feelings. He apologized with downcast eyes as we drank coffee in a cafe on Geary Boulevard. He informed me he was going to wait until October to move, because of a project he had to finish for his employer.

In September, I packed my life into the trunk of my car and left San Francisco for the bright lights of New York. As the last San Francisco seminar approached, I knew I had made the right choice to move. With the love affair officially over, nothing in the Bay Area was that important to me anymore. The people and places didn't sparkle with the light I craved. I wanted to live in worlds of miracles and magic, and the only one I had met who could teach me how to reach those worlds was Rama.

Katey had already moved to New York with her computer certificate, ready to hit the pavement and find work in Manhattan. At a previous seminar, Tanya had introduced me to her friend Lloyd, who said I could stay with him and his roommate since they already had a house set up in Connecticut. Never before did I feel so supported about a decision. Even though I hardly knew these people, our practice of meditation pulled us together so we could aid each other in our move to the Big Apple.

The final sign I received before leaving was a call from my high school friend Melony. She had started attending Rama's classes in Los Angeles, after I hooked her up with a mentor through Tara. She called to tell me she had decided to move to New York with the rest of us, but she couldn't drive across with me. I gave her the voicemail number I had set up and told her to meet me at Lloyd's house in Connecticut.

Late on Saturday morning, I cruised over the Bay Bridge on my way out of San Francisco listening to Zazen. The image of Rama glowing on the small stage I had seen him on the previous night burned in my mind. In just one week, I would see him again when I began my new life in New York. The golden hills of California zipped past me as I sped down the highway, thinking of Rama's talk about being alone.

"There's a difference between aloneness and loneliness," he said compassionately to the small group of students who were still left in San Francisco. "Everyone gets lonely sometimes. It's a normal human emotion. So that's why I have Scottie dogs, the best friends you could ever have. As long as you take care of them, they'll never hurt you. They're completely innocent creatures. But some people feel lonely all of the time, even among their friends, because they haven't accepted the fact we are all ultimately alone in the universe.

"Being alone is a simple fact of life. You were born alone into this world, and you'll die alone. It's not good or bad; that's just the way it is. I find it very freeing to know I'm alone, because it means I'm not responsible for anyone except myself. It relieves the burden so many people carry around all of their life, thinking they have to please everyone else.

"It can be frightening to realize you're alone in this tremendous universe, to realize no one cares because they're all on their own trip. But I find it refreshing that no one really cares, because when you fully realize this, you don't have to make justifications to anyone, not even to yourself. You can do what feels right for you without checking with anyone else. Your actions become more fluid and in tune with the natural flow of the universe. You don't have to impose any ideas of what is right and what is wrong on your actions. You do things because it's right for the moment, not because it's right for some abstract reason," continued Rama.

"Loneliness, however, is a passing phase like all emotions. You shouldn't let it rule you, but don't deny it either. If you feel lonely, pet your Scottie dog, or call a friend, go see a movie, or read an uplifting book. Just don't wallow in it; instead do something.

"If you feel lonely all of the time, though, it could be because you're hiding from the fact that you are alone," said Rama. "Part of becoming spiritually mature is accepting that people will come and go in your life, but you'll always be left with yourself, alone in your own world of plans, dreams, and schemes."

As I left California, I knew I was leaving behind many people I would never see again. My friends at school and the bar were all sad when we said good-bye, but the light in my heart kept me from feelings of melancholy. For me, this adventure I had undertaken alone, was one of the most important steps in my life. This time, as I began my next life-changing journey, I wasn't waiting for anyone else.

The sun sank into the brown smog line that hung over the Pacific, creating a glorious burst of red, pink and orange as I left California. Behind the wheel of my Nissan I felt so alive and free, like a soaring eagle, with the cool wind rushing through my hair. I could feel the magic of life all around me as I crossed over into a whole new world.

In the morning, a sign for Zion National Park invited me to take a tour of the forests of Utah. The sun beamed through the trees, splashing shadows onto the ominous red mountains that appeared like massive rocks on fire. I hiked up a trail lined with greenery leading to the Emerald Pools, where the water gathered in deep stone basins before running over the cliff to a lake below. I found a partially secluded place behind a few struggling trees to meditate. On the other side of the trees surrounding the boulder I sat on, people shuffled by, but the music from my walkman and the running stream drowned the noise and allowed me to slip into Zazen.

Near the close of my meditation, I felt a presence focusing on me. I opened my eyes to see a woman staring at me with a bewildered expression. I smiled at her politely, knowing it probably wasn't very often a Buddhist monk was found meditating in Utah. Embarrassed, she quickly looked away and followed her friend down the trail. I finished my meditation with a bow, and continued my hike through the park.

I arrived back at my car at sunset, but there was still one more place I wanted to see before I left Zion: the Temple of Sinawave. It was at the end of the paved road that ran through the park, so I decided to take a quick drive down there. The two mile drive, however, felt more like ten as a menacing feeling overwhelmed me. I scolded myself for being so ridiculous, convinced I was unreasonably afraid of being alone in the woods after dark.

I parked in front of the restrooms, intending to take a short stroll around the area before the sunlight was completely gone. But something inside me kept nagging, almost begging me to leave as quickly as possible. I ignored the feeling, until I stepped out of the car. My body just didn't want to hike in that area. My feet felt like cement blocks and I kept glancing over my shoulder. Finally, I decided just to use the ladies' room and leave.

On the way back to my car, I spotted a small tourist information plaque. It informed me the local Indian tribe had named the area after their benevolent wolf-god, and they would never stay in that particular gorge after sunset because of evil forces. That small incident gave me a new respect for my intuition, and I vowed to never again ignore such strong feelings.

The next day, I toured the northern rim of the Grand Canyon that stretches through Arizona. Although many of the paths were crowded, the immense beauty of this natural sculpture could not be diminished. Pure tranquility soaked through me as I viewed the spectacular form of stone, space, and tree.

Off the beaten trail along the rim, I found a cliff of smooth stones, jutting out into the emptiness where I meditated in silence. The wind whipped through the Canyon, extinguishing both the voices and the aura of the people, cutting down to the core of my being. This wind, that had smoothed the walls of the Canyon, tore through the illusions of my mind, taking me to new unexplored heights. In contrast to Zion, I felt completely safe, as if I could stay on that ledge for all eternity.

This magnificent dreamland where the sidewalk ends teased me with its lures of perfect serenity. I wanted to stay, melt into the stones and become one with all of this. I slowly drifted into lazy contentment, basking in the sun.

The cry of a hawk jolted me suddenly, reminding me of the transient nature of this world and waking me up to the true purpose of my journey: Enlightenment. Drawing in a deep breath, I scanned the horizon one last time, planting memories for inspiration on the difficult days that undoubtedly lay ahead. Reluctantly, I drove out the Canyon, tearing myself free of its magnet-like pull.

The Painted Desert outside of the Grand Canyon greeted me at twilight with all of the warmth of a psychopathic murderer. Never before had I felt so much fear coursing through my body and soul. The night closed around me like a hangman's noose, making the dread I felt at sunset in Zion a soft summer's rain in comparison. Even the starlight seemed to die out before reaching the ground. Everything was pitch black as I traveled down the two-lane highway. It seemed to be the only road in the area and there was not another car for miles and miles.

Recalling the warrior beings from the last desert trip with Rama, I silently asked that they protect me as I passed through this desolate land of Indian ruins. Sleep attempted to choke me, but the sight of the matchbox towns I drove through spurned me forward, away from the unseen horrors I could feel reeking in the air. My only solace was found by munching on the graham crackers I had stashed in the glove compartment and by singing at the top of my lungs to the tapes I had brought. A sign for the southern rim of the Grand Canyon jarred memories of its security and nearly made me turn. I forced myself to stay on my chosen path, regardless of the dangers I would have to face before finding rest in a hotel room.

I continued my battle against the desire to sleep until I reached Flagstaff, where I found a room to recuperate in. I was completely drained from my experience, but I had also pulled up some weird power reserve that had me totally wired. Fortunately, the hotel had a hot tub, where I soaked until I unwound enough to meditate and sleep.

The following morning, as I rolled along Interstate 40 into New Mexico, déjà-vu invaded my body and grew stronger with every passing mile. I had never been to New Mexico, but the thought was always in the back of my mind, often forgotten, that I would someday travel in that state. A slight pressure in my navel chakra made me aware of the power in that area, but I couldn't quite grasp what was happening to me.

At the edge of the plains, tears of joy sprang from my eyes. I felt like I had found my home after being lost for many years, and the things that were once precious to me were being returned. Crosby, Stills, and Nash's *Deja-vu* played on the radio, adding to the mystical feeling that had overcome me. The feeling of falling in love embraced me like a spring flood, lifting me into a state of ecstasy. The colors of the sand sparkled like jewels on a crown underneath the clear blue sky, stretching into the horizon where they joined like lovers in a slow sensual dance.

Crossing the plains, the pressure on my navel intensified, shifting me into a more profound state of awareness. These strange and intangible gifts of power I was receiving in the second attention were accompanied by a major sense of responsibility, but I had no clue how to use this endowment. The question of what I was supposed to do kept ringing in my head, but my intuition kept leading me back to Rama. I had to ask him to teach me something, but what exactly that thing was I could not articulate.

I pulled off the road several times to gaze at the mesas in the north, almost expecting to see Rama. I could feel his presence, and if I closed my eyes, I could see his eyes shining clear blue, like the sky over the desert. Questions about the power of the desert, and how could I use it to move further along the pathway to Enlightenment rang in my mind. I pushed my little red car to go faster. I couldn't wait to talk to Rama, and hoped that by the time I saw him, I would know how to ask these questions and that I would understand the answers.

THE INVITATION

The stars meditate constantly.
They burn their very substance
To give Light to others.
This is constant and conscious meditation.
                                    -Rama

While in my car, miles away from Rama, it was easy for me to imagine talking to him. When it came my moment to ask for his assistance in my quest for knowledge, however, I found out I was a bigger coward than I had ever realized. During the breaks at the two September seminars I had rushed across country to attend, I watched him from a distance. He moved gracefully through the crowd of students, answering question after question, always smiling. New Mexico kept flashing in my mind, but there were no words. He walked by, eyeing me curiously, as if he were waiting for me to approach him with my questions. Unfortunately, I found myself speechless every time he came near.

Melony arrived in New York during October and joined me at Lloyd's house. Melony and I relived our high school memories; it was like a reunion of sisters as we talked about the days of our past and planned for the future. Neither one of us had very much money, so we decided to find an apartment together.

I found work through a temporary agency doing word-processing, and she picked up a waitressing job. By putting our money together, we found a two-bedroom apartment within a week that we could both afford. After we settled into our new place, I bought a computer with my credit card, finally making the commitment to learn something from the computer classes Rama was offering as part of the study.

At the seminars, I noticed Rama walking by me during the breaks as my friends and I shared stories about our journey across country. I thought I was just being paranoid, until Lloyd confirmed that Rama had looked at me more than once while I was standing in our usual group. I couldn't understand why I was so nervous about talking to Rama. I wanted to ask him about New Mexico, but every time he came near me I would run away.

On Thanksgiving, Rama held a banquet at Tappan Hill in Westchester to celebrate the holiday. Since most of the students were vegetarians, he served fish and vegetable dishes as well as the traditional turkey. I thought it was interesting so many of my peers were also vegetarians. Rama had never told us to not eat meat. He only stated once how meat can make you feel heavy, and suggested we don't eat too much red meat because of the health consequences. Most of the people I talked to, however, had become vegetarians before meeting

Rama. Many of them, like me, had simply lost the taste for meat.

At the end of the seminar, Melony told me to wait for her because Rama had asked her to stay to talk to him. At first I was simply curious, but as time passed, I became more and more jealous. After all, he had been looking at me during the breaks; why didn't he want to talk to me too? I sat by myself, concentrating on writing a poem about the flower arrangement on the table. I knew it was beyond rude to be angry that Rama chose to talk to Melony and not to me. As I sat there, I thought about Rama's talk earlier in the evening about the importance of feeling gratitude every day, not just on Thanksgiving.

During the ride home, Melony wouldn't budge an inch about what Rama had said to her. I didn't ask her outwardly, but I made it clear as I drove that I expected her to tell me something. Finally, after a long silence, I relented by telling her I had no choice but to respect her decision not to share what she and Rama had talked about.

In December, I saw Rama from across the room walking towards me. I immediately ducked into the crowd and started talking to the first person I saw. When she walked away, I went to the ladies room to fix my hair and lipstick. As I entered the banquet room, I heard Rama saying hello behind me when no one else was in hearing range. I had no choice but to talk to him then; there was no escape. Even though I had been waiting months for this opportunity, feelings of fear continued to rush through me.

Rama asked me my name and where I worked.

His small talk made me feel more comfortable, but my thoughts and questions raced out of my mind before I could catch them. He patiently waited for me to find the words, as I tried to descramble my brain.

"I'm sorry," I finally said, "whenever I come near you, my mind goes blank."

"That's okay," he said gently. "It happens. Just try to relax. Do you live alone?"

"No, I have a roommate, Melony. We've known each other for years."

"So, what did you want to ask me?" Rama looked at me intently.

"When I drove through New Mexico," I began slowly as I forced my mouth to form words. "I had the strangest sensation in my navel center. It was like someone was pressing on it. And I had the feeling like I was supposed to ask you how to do something."

"You were feeling the power of that state. It's a very strong area," he answered, looking directly into my eyes.

The rest of the room disappeared and I felt as if I were alone with him in infinity, suspended in space. We exchanged a few more words, but I couldn't come up with the questions I really wanted to ask. I simply did not know what those questions were. I only knew I wanted to keep talking to him. At one time he had been an English professor, so I asked if he would critique some poems I had written, hoping he would be willing to work with me as a writer.

I began to feel extremely light-headed when he stopped speaking for a moment and looked away silently. Suddenly, I felt very awkward standing there. I didn't know what to do with myself, whether I should say something, walk away, or just wait patiently. The safest thing to do was to stay put, so I politely looked away from him and waited for him to resume the conversation.

"So you want to spend some time with me then," he stated flatly after what seemed like hours.

"Well, yes," I blurted out abruptly.

"Fine, then. Why don't you come to my house on Sunday. And bring a couple of changes of clothes, just something casual like jeans or whatever."

I must have looked dumbfounded because he added, "That is what you wanted, right?"

"Yes, yes definitely," I replied, swallowing my shock at the invitation.

"We'll get you directions tomorrow night at the seminar. You probably shouldn't tell your roommate, because people have the tendency to be jealous," he commented.

"OK," I said, feeling slightly faint.

He smiled and walked away. As I looked around, the room came flooding back. For a while, I had been completely oblivious that I was in a roomful of people and that it was nearly midnight on New Year's Eve.

HOME WITH THE ENLIGHTENED

Words are only shells.
Win conviction of God's presence
Through your own joyous contact
In meditation.
                              -Lahiri Mahasaya

I drove into the twilight, arriving at Rama's house at 7 o'clock, as he had suggested. After ringing the buzzer, the wooden gate swung open from the middle, revealing a stone lane lined with pagoda lanterns. As I turned up the driveway, I felt as if I was entering another world where my petty cares and worries didn't matter. The gate closed, blending in with the tall shrubbery and sealing the grounds from the intrusions of the public.

I caught my breath as I examined the elegant design of the house. Its roofs had sweeping angles like the pagoda lanterns of the driveway, reminding me of the architecture of the sacred temples in the Far East. Light poured from the glass walls onto the snow-covered lawn as one black and two blond Scottie dogs rushed to greet me. I recognized Vayu, the black dog, from one of the seminars Rama had hosted in Marin.

Rama met me at the door with a broad smile and asked me to leave my shoes there, as was the custom in Asian homes. I followed him first to a guest room, where I left my bag, and then he gave me a short tour of his home. Thangkas of various Bodhisattvas hung in every room, constantly pulling my mind towards the mystery of Enlightenment.

A thousand different feelings rushed through me. The strongest was of sheer terror. For no rational reason, I wanted to run out of there as fast as I could. Then it hit me that I had nowhere to go. I had traveled through most of the country, gone to college, and looked for a husband. I had already tried all of the things I thought would make me happy and they didn't work. Now I was at home with the happiest person I had ever met, and he was willing to teach me some of what he knew. Realistically, I simply had nothing left to lose.

We meditated in the living room that evening, with only the crackling fire breaking the silence. Red, indigo, and gold swallowed the room as my very being dissolved. Nothing was solid as my fears and expectations evaporated into the ether. I could not see Rama, yet I sensed his presence as a gentle wave of pure light flowing all around me. I wanted to stay in that kaleidoscope forever, but soon we were back, sitting on the shag rug in front of the fireplace.

I looked at him in amazement, hoping he would tell me what just happened. Instead, he smiled and said we should get some sleep.

The next morning, some of my self-consciousness had left me and I was able to say a few words to Rama without feeling like a complete idiot. He made a few jokes to put me at ease while I drank my coffee, but I continued to remain stupefied by the fact I was actually in his house.

"You'll notice I'm always straightening things here," he said in a soft tone as he carefully arranged the shoes I had thoughtlessly slipped off the night before.

"When you put things in place with proper intent, you literally support your environment."

"What's proper intent?" I interrupted rudely.

"It means you focus on what you're doing with a purpose," he replied patiently, letting me know with a look that I shouldn't interrupt him again.

"When you arrange the things in your home or office, you extend your aura out around you, and it keeps others from being able to intrude on an energy level. It's always good to keep things neat and clean," he reiterated. "So when you meditate, you're not sitting in someone else's energy. It's hard enough to stop your own thoughts, never mind everyone else's, right?"

"Yeah," I agreed, thinking of the clothes and books strewn about my room at home.

"Your external environment is really a reflection on your state of awareness. Occultists are always focused on what they are doing, so their homes are always immaculate, with everything lined up. If on the other hand, your house is messy with stuff everywhere, your mind is probably pretty scattered."

I nodded in agreement, realizing how badly I

needed to get my act together.

"Occultists deal with energy. In the same way that you lock doors to keep people from coming in, occultists extend their energy around them to block out others on a psychic level. The study of Buddhism is all about conserving energy. This is what Buddhist etiquette teaches you; it's a way of living a bright, tight life. Physically, we don't really do much. We just live simple, quiet lives, minding our own business and keeping things in order.

"Meditation is really a private inner study," continued Rama. "It's about transformation and going to other worlds that are deeper and more profound than what you can find out there," he said, waving his hand towards the street.

It would have been easy to sit there and listen to him all day, but he decided that it would be better to meditate and run a few errands.

I shoved my hands deeper into the pockets of my denim jacket as the frosty January wind hit my face. I was in debt from moving and couldn't afford a new jacket, so I had bundled up with an extra sweater, but it wasn't enough.

"Are you making a fashion statement or do you need a coat?" asked Rama as he noticed me shiver.

"I need a coat," I said, embarrassed that I wasn't prepared for the winter.

"We'll have to get you one while we're here," said Rama as we headed into Macy's.

"The best way to shop," he continued, "is to know what you need, find the most high-vibe product, and leave as quickly as possible. You don't want to be standing in the aisle gawking at everything, because you'll start picking up on everyone else's thoughts and you might start buying things you don't even want."

I had to stretch my legs to keep up with his long, easy stride. His every motion was done with precision and speed; nothing could deter him from his goal.

"Do you want to study the occult under me?" he asked suddenly.

"Yes," I replied, looking at him eagerly.

"Then always walk on the right side. Remember what don Juan said in the Castaneda books?" He gazed into my eyes with such intensity I felt my awareness shift as we walked past the racks of clothing.

"Yes," I answered confidently, but at the same time scolding myself for not acting on what I knew. "He said that Death is on the left."

"So you don't want to get in its way, right?"

"No, I don't," I answered, stepping quickly to his right side.

"Stand up straighter. If you want to be a warrior, you'll have to start acting like one. You don't want to look like a push over, because people will take advantage of you," he explained as I put my shoulders back. "It's an adversarial world. People are out to get what they can, however they can.

"You don't want to make yourself a target by looking like a lost little girl with that spacey look in your eyes," continued Rama. "You always want to be focused and know exactly what you're doing and where you're going, so people don't bother you. It's called being inaccessible. You blend into your surroundings and do what you need to do."

As we left Macy's and entered the main mall area, I noticed a few teenage girls with the spacey look that Rama had talked about. I hardened my expression and stuck close to his side.

"Let's try to spot an occultist while we're here," he suggested as we cruised past a stand selling hand-made jewelry.

"It's not easy because good occultists will never reveal themselves. They like to blend into the crowd because interactions with people can be very costly on an energy level."

"How can someone drain you that easily?" I asked.

"When you connect with someone, you go into their aura and pull whatever mind states they happen to be in into you," explained Rama. "Say you're walking along enjoying the view, happy in your own little world. Then you notice a couple fighting and you lock onto their conversation with your mind. Suddenly, you start feeling angry for no apparent reason, and if you don't catch yourself, you could waste your beautiful day by carrying that anger around. Then the little things that normally wouldn't bother you start throwing you off balance, and you may even get into a fight. By the time you get home, you're completely drained, all because you focused on them when they were in that mind set."

"If they blend so well, how can you pick out an occultist?" I inquired, anxious to get on with the game.

"By their eyes," he said nonchalantly.

"What you mean, the eyes?" I asked again with more interest.

"They have a sharp, cold look of total indifference. They're very focused and strong."

I followed him through the mall, glancing at the people. I didn't know what I was looking for, so I waited for his lead. We stopped at B. Dalton's, where he picked up a magazine with three women on the cover.

"Which one is the occultist?" he asked, catching me off-guard.

"This one," I said pointing on instinct to a pretty blond with green eyes.

"Right," said Rama. "It takes a lot of power to be one of these super models, or to succeed in Hollywood. She knows how to conserve energy and push it out when she needs to; she's an occultist. That's why you noticed her first. She's got more power than the other two."

He put the magazine down and headed for the door. I figured my lesson was over, so I let myself relax.

"She didn't look very happy, huh?" Rama asked quietly, pulling me back from my window shopping.

"No, not really, but it could have just been the pose for all I know," I admitted weakly.

"She had some power, but power doesn't make you happy," he continued outside the bookstore. "A lot of people go after power, after money that is. You know that, right? Money, especially in this country, is a symbol of power."

I nodded in agreement, thinking about all of the things I could do if I had the money.

"But most people get obsessive and they just keep wanting more power and more money, even though it's not taking them anywhere," he continued. "They forget that anything else exists and it swallows them. Some people reach a point where they have so much of it, they don't know what to do with it, and it eventually destroys them. It seems like such a waste, but people are people and they have to go through whatever karma they set up. You need power to go into higher states of awareness, where you can experience more dimensions, but it's not power itself that brings happiness."

We then headed into an Eddie Bauer store, where Rama loaded my arms with sweaters and socks and a bright purple winter coat. At the register, he handed me four hundred dollar bills and told me he'd meet me in front of the store.

I didn't know why he waited outside while I paid for the clothes, and my heart raced as I handed him the change. Rama smiled when he saw me put on the new coat, which fit perfectly, and we left the mall without a word.

The following day, Rama took me to a power spot near his house. As we sat silently looking out at the water, I could see thin dark lines stretching across Long Island Sound.

"People connect to each other through energy lines," he told me. In my heightened state of awareness, everything was perfectly clear to me. It seemed as if I knew what he was going to say just before he said it, but if he had asked me, I would not have been able to find words to express all that I was feeling. The sound of his voice kept me from getting lost in all the different sensations as I watched the waves.

"The lines you see over the water are energy lines between people. That's one of the reasons why the world feels so heavy to people who are open psychically," explained Rama. "We're constantly being bombarded by human aura. Most people, however, are totally unaware of how much energy they throw around. All of these lines form complex webs that are easy to get tangled in if you don't watch yourself."

"How do you cut the energy lines you have with someone?" I asked, as thoughts of my ex-boyfriend Larry kept intruding on the silence of my mind.

"Just be indifferent towards them," Rama answered simply.

"But how do I do it without numbing myself to everything. I can block them out, but then I can't feel anything at all," I complained.

"You can numb yourself to one person or thing, without shutting off your feelings completely. You just focus on something else," he said gently. "Love comes with hurt, but you have to be strong and push through that hurt, and love something else.

"When something hurts you, the only intelligent thing to do is to let go of it. Don't hate it, because that will tie you to it and burn up even more energy. Remember, before you loved it, you didn't have any feelings for it. So, you just go back to that indifference."

He looked at me with clear blue eyes filled with compassion. As I looked into them, I felt myself slip away from the world of sorrow and anger. My rage towards Larry vanished as I forgave him for the times he cheated on me in San Francisco. Suddenly, I felt released from our failed relationship and my heart grew lighter. In that moment, there was only joy, pure innocent joy.

"You can love a surprisingly great number of people and things if you let yourself," he added, as I turned my gaze to the water. "That's where happiness comes from. It comes from loving, not from being loved. Even if the whole world loved you, it wouldn't make a difference if you didn't love something in return.

"You have to understand, love is an energy that flows through you when you give it to someone or something," continued Rama. "It's not something you can bottle up and keep for yourself. It's energy, it has to flow.

"But remember, everything in this world is transitory, so when whatever you love starts to hurt you, you have to let it go. If you try to hold on when it's not right, then you start to resent what you once loved and you won't feel love anymore. Instead, you'll feel anger and resentment and pain. It's when you give up that attachment, that you're free to put your love into something else. So, you don't ever have to stop loving."

As he said these few simple words to me, I felt my heart open. After I left San Francisco, I had locked my heart behind walls of steel, refusing to let myself really care about anyone. When Matthew had arrived in New York, I had given him my phone number in a vain attempt to rekindle the passion we had felt. When he didn't call, it made the walls around my heart stronger. After listening to

Rama, I clearly saw my pattern of clinging to men like Matthew and Larry. These men were able to spark passion within me but were not able to follow through with a commitment. Creating relationships with these types of men was my way of avoiding real emotions. I realized it wasn't protection I needed. What I really needed was control of my emotional longings.

The next day as I was leaving his house, Rama said to me, "Your challenge is to keep yourself sharp and aware and at the same time be relaxed. When you're around me, I feel everything you feel and think, so try not to be so uptight."

As I looked at him to say thank you, I was overwhelmed by the impression I had known him at some earlier time I could not remember. There was no way for me to tell him what I felt without sounding foolish, so I simply smiled on my way out the door and went back to my world in Westchester.

THE JOY OF SCOTTIE DOGS

The way is not in the sky.
The way is in the heart.
                              -The Dhammapada

At home the next morning, Melony looked at me inquisitively, but never said a word. I simply told her I had met someone and decided to stay with him for a while. She accepted this, since it was something she had done many times before during her travels.

A few weeks later, while watching a movie after work, the phone rang, causing us both to jump.

"Hello," answered Melony politely, reminding me of the receptionist at an office.

"Who's calling? I'll have to check. Who's calling, please," she demanded. Obviously it was for me, but she wanted to know who it was before giving up the phone. I looked at her and put out my hand for the receiver.

"He won't tell me who it is, and he sounds really angry," she said indignantly with her hand over the mouthpiece. I really didn't care that she

113

had asked, but it did make me nervous that the person on the other line had refused her request.

"Subtly is a lost art, huh?" said the voice on the other end.

"Uh, yeah," I answered walking into my bedroom, trying to figure out who was on the phone.

"So, how's the purple coat?" he joked. "I called your voice mail, but since you didn't return my call, I figured I'd try the direct approach."

"Great!" I said, finally realizing it was Rama on the phone. "We were watching *Dracula*, so I haven't checked my messages for a while."

"I need you to come down tomorrow night to dog-sit for a few days."

"Sure. I'll have to take the train out there. My car is frozen and I think it's pretty much dead," I answered, excited by the idea of visiting Rama's home again so soon.

"I figured the last time you were here it didn't have much life in it. It's probably a long ride, so check the schedule. You should get here around eleven tomorrow morning. The train station isn't far from my house, so I'll pick you up." After a brief pause, Rama continued, "She's pretty angry, so watch your back."

"You think so?" I asked hesitantly, as it clicked in my mind that he was talking about Melony. "I don't think she knows anything."

"She probably doesn't, but she *feels* something going on. That's why she was so insistent on the phone. She's trying to figure it out."

I hung up the phone feeling wary of my roommate, wondering how she would react if she found out I had been to Rama's house. As I walked back into the living room, she gave me her customary grin and pushed the bowl of popcorn towards me.

The next morning, Rama picked me up a few minutes after the train left me at the station. The ride had taken several hours, and had given me a chance to read *The Hobbit*, a novel Rama had suggested all his students read shortly after I had arrived in New York.

"You're hungry, huh?" asked Rama as he pulled into the small restaurant across from the train station.

"Yeah, I guess a little," I answered slowly, not really sure if I wanted to eat.

"Well, right now you're feeling a bit disoriented, but food will settle you down."

I had to admit he was right. On the train I had felt completely in control and aware, but now that I was with Rama, I felt lost. We sat in the restaurant and I was surprised to hear Zazen playing. Rama explained he had given the owner a few CD's, so they usually put one on when they saw him.

Once at the house, he led me towards the guest rooms. The last time I was there, I had slept in the smaller room which was accented with violet curtains. I had chosen it because purple was my favorite color, but this time I felt like trying the other room. It was accented with orange and one wall was mirrored, making the 8x10 room appear even larger.

As I put my bag down in the orange room, Rama looked at me inquisitively and asked, "You want to stay in here this time?"

"Yeah," I answered, wondering if I had done something wrong. "I like variety, so I thought I'd try out this room. And I also want to be able to exercise when I get up. This room has more space for that."

"Oh, that's fine. I just want you to feel the difference between the two. You just got off the train, so you might not be able to tell right now, but come here," he said, leading me into the purple room. "Notice how this feels," he continued as we stood for a moment in the smaller room. "And now come in here." I followed him across the hall to the orange room.

"This one seems more public," I said, trying to think of a better word. "Maybe because it's more open."

"Come here again," he said, pulling me back into the purple room. I was beginning to feel silly walking back and forth between rooms, and bit my tongue to keep from laughing. "This one feels more like the ocean, don't you think?"

I agreed, noticing how much quieter it seemed.

"The other room faces the road, so it is more public. You can feel the world more in there than you can in here. When I sleep downstairs, I like this room better, but the bed is too short for my legs. I had to have it made that way so it would fit in here. But you're welcome to stay in the other room. It'll be interesting for you to see the difference."

On his way out the door for his trip to Boston, Rama knelt down to pet each of the Scottie dogs, beginning with Vayu.

"You're a number two dog," said Rama as he pushed Karma, one of the blond dogs, away from Vayu. Karma kept coming back for more attention.

"Even if Vayu wasn't here, you'd still be a number two dog," joked Rama as I watched him play with Vayu and ignore Karma. India, the other blond dog, sat patiently next to him.

I knew the dogs were his true loves in life, especially Vayu. Rama checked one more time that I had the number to the vet and the security guard he hired to check on the house before leaving to meet his intermediate students.

I spent the evening playing with the three Scottie dogs and reading *The Hobbit*. Each of the dogs had his own personality, and all of them loved the attention. India would play catch with the plastic frogs Rama had bought for them, sliding across the wooden floor. Vayu would walk around me in circles as I petted him, and Karma would get jealous and stand right in front of me if I spent too much time playing with the others.

I watched movies the next day as snow began falling from the sky. The dogs ran around the yard, and would come inside every hour or two to jump on me with their wet fur. I spent most of the day wiping up the melted snow from the floor, and laughing as they chased each other around the house.

As night settled in, the dogs fell asleep scattered around me on the couch. I noticed my neck had been hurting all day as I rubbed it. I turned my head to stretch the muscles, but nothing relived the tension. I did my best to ignore the pain while reading my book.

Rama came home in the middle of the night, setting the dogs off in a major barking spree and jolting me out of my half-asleep-half-reading state.

The snow had nearly kept him in Boston, but it had lightened up by the end of the seminar so he was able to drive home.

We stayed up talking and eating cookies until sunrise, when the early morning birds began screeching their hellos to the world.

"So you can feel her now, huh?" asked Rama as I rubbed my neck again.

"What do you mean?"

"That pain you're feeling. It's your roommate. She's pissed off at you," said Rama, taking a bite of another cookie.

"Really?" I asked, not wanting to believe that Melony would actually attack me psychically.

"Who keeps popping into your mind?"

"Melony," I admitted weakly.

"Right. Now, push her out," he commanded, locking his eyes with mine. "Don't let her slam you like that because if you just stand there and take it, she'll keep on doing it every time you do something she doesn't like."

I imagined pushing her out of my mind, and the pain ceased for a moment, and then came back again stronger.

"You can always tell who's attacking you psychically because when you focus on them, they back off. But if you don't fight it, they'll hit you again harder. There are no friends after high school," he said sternly.

"I just can't believe she would be so petty. I mean, I thought we were working together and helping each other out," I whined. "That's why we decided to live together. We used to have so much fun together, but now everything's a competition," I continued, thinking about the last conversation I had with Melony about computers. She spent most of her free time teaching herself to write programs on my computer, while I used the temporary jobs I picked up to increase my skills. When I landed my first assignment in a computer department, she insisted she would get a better job than mine once she learned to write code.

"People get jealous and they deal with it in their own way. You have to be tough if you want to hang out around me. So keep her out of your head. She's a little out of control, but she's not stupid."

I left the next day feeling stronger, but disappointed that my best friend wanted to hurt me. I never liked fighting very much; I had had enough of it growing up in a large family. In the past I would always let my friends have their way rather than fight it out, but this was taking it too far.

When I got home, I confronted Melony about slamming me psychically. She pretended at first not to understand what I was talking about, and then she simply denied it. After the clash, she left the room pouting.

We avoided each other for the next few weeks as things settled down. I continued to pick up temporary jobs doing word processing and had managed to pick up the occasional software trainer position to pay the rent, while Melony continued to waitress.

Finally, we called a truce, and I asked her why she didn't get an office job. Temporary work paid about the same, and it wasn't as draining as serving hungry people all day. She understood what I meant about being drained and asked if I had any leads. I called one of my agencies and sent Melony over to talk to them. The next week she had an assignment as a receptionist and bought her first suit for the office.

Later in the week I was offered a job in a computer department restructuring their help desk. Excited about the new contract, I told Melony about it when she came home that night. After my evening meditation I drifted off to sleep, knowing I would have to get up early to make it into Manhattan on time.

I woke up suddenly, aware of pressure all over my body. I opened my eyes, but nothing seemed out of the ordinary, so I let myself drift back into sleep. I was at that stage of just falling to sleep when I sensed Melony attacking me again. I didn't want to deal with it, but I knew she meant to seriously injure me this time, not just give me a pain in the neck. I was more annoyed than angry, so I imagined a wall of mirrors protecting my body. She kept coming at me full force, so I took the mirrors and pointed them at her ankle. I watched the energy reflect straight back towards her and then it suddenly stopped.

I opened my eyes again, wondering if what I experienced had just been a dream of pure imagination. I wanted to believe it had been a fantasy, but it had all seemed so real.

I woke up in the morning refreshed and excited about my new job. While eating breakfast, I heard Melony stirring in her room. A few minutes later, I heard a loud bang and a muffled curse. I sat silently for a moment, knowing perfectly well that last night's events had not been a mere dream.

"Are you OK?" I called from the kitchen when I didn't hear any more movement.

"Yeah," answered Melony, limping into the kitchen. "I stood up after meditating and my ankle just gave out. But I think it'll be all right in a few minutes."

Too freaked out to say anything, I washed my dishes and finished getting ready for work. Slowly it dawned on me that all this talk of energy and power was about something very real.

Rama's warnings about being careful with the power we were gaining rang in my mind. He had told me to protect myself, but there had to be a better way than throwing the energy back at the attacker, no matter who it was. I had won last night's battle, but I knew I was in danger of getting sucked into an occult war and losing my dream of Enlightenment forever.

YOGA IS HARMONY

The ocean is Life.
No part of it remains constant,
Yet as a whole it is still.
The ocean absorbs all resistance -
The crashing waves are its only release,
And even they recoil
And drain back into the sea.

The icy winter killed Melony's car shortly after mine died, so we had to rely on our mutual friends to drive us to the computer seminars every other weekend. Forced laughter often punctuated the ride as Melony and I pretended to joke about the tension we felt. We blamed the world for our pain, and spent our time complaining about the amount of reading the mentors gave us between seminars. Our friends soon learned to ignore us by popping in an Zazen tape and turning up the volume.

Once we arrived at the hall, we would go our separate ways until it was time to leave. I missed laughing with her and the intimacy of a long friendship, but I didn't want to open myself up to her because I was afraid she would attack me again.

Although Rama was not physically present at the computer seminars, the room vibrated with the same energy as if he were meditating in front of us. The intermediate students, many who had been studying with Rama for over twelve years, taught the classes with humor and excitement. The classes lasted for over six hours each day, but they always ended before I lost interest. I never imagined learning about corporate power structures and systems design could be so much fun as they made jokes tied in perfectly with the concepts they were teaching.

The material covered in the four classes each month would have taken at least a full semester in any traditional university, but somehow, even at that advanced rate, I was able to absorb and understand the subjects. If I stopped to think about how much information was being given to me, I would feel overwhelmed and want to leave the room. But once I relaxed and learned to take everything one step at a time, the concepts were deceptively simple. Over time, we learned not only the technical issues of relational database design and computer programming, but also the finer points of how to dress for the corporate world and how to write resumes for different types of positions.

At the computer classes, and especially during the seminars Rama gave personally, I would catch myself feeling egotistical because of my close relationship with Rama. I was fully aware Rama had similar personal relationships with students other than me, but I would often catch myself feeling somehow special compared to the others in the study.

One evening while waiting for Rama to walk out on stage, I looked around the hall and realized everyone there was unique and special in his or her own way. Everyone had their own talent, their own gift they brought into the world to make it a brighter place. As I watched the people, I noticed how different each one was compared to the next, knowing I was different than anyone else, but not in any way better.

"Tonight let's talk about what is yoga," said Rama as he made himself comfortable in the chair at center stage.

"Yoga is meditation. By meditating, you move into a higher state of consciousness. In your solitary practice, you will eventually reach a plateau. So, the next step is to find a teacher to take you higher.

"The interesting thing about the study of meditation is there is always another level to reach," he continued. "Enlightenment goes on forever into infinity. What a teacher will show you is how to streamline your life in order to conserve energy, so when you do sit in meditation, you have the power to reach deeper into the light.

"And by meditating with an Enlightened teacher, you will learn things in the second attention, which are the things that cannot be spoken. These are the secrets that are mentioned in some of the Eastern writings you've read. The ancient texts often refer to this as the transmission of light. When you meditate with an Enlightened teacher, you are actually receiving the light that manifests when they meditate. This light will open doorways into higher dimensions that you would not be able to reach alone. The idea behind meditating with an advanced teacher is that with practice, the student learns how to get to these places on their own."

My mind was silent as the hall filled with the golden light emanating from Rama.

"Yoga means union. It is harmony. To practice yoga means to find the balance within yourself," continued Rama. "Think of it this way: Everyone likes the water during their shower a certain temperature. In life, we seek to find the temperature that feels good to us. The way you can find this balance, or ideal temperature, is to quiet your mind and just listen. The deeper part of your being always knows what is right for you. Whenever you have an important decision to make, ask yourself right after you meditate, since that's when your mind is the clearest.

"By practicing yoga, we learn that we have options. We learn that we don't have to live in a world of sadness and pain. Meditation clears our vision and allows us to see the universe as it really is: a place of extraordinary beauty. Imagine driving in a car with a dirty windshield – that's how most people see life. Their vision is clouded by negative thoughts, so they can't see where they're going. By practicing yoga, by meditating and paying attention to your thoughts throughout the day, you clean the windshield. Then you can see what's in front of you and prepare accordingly," said Rama, pulling his sunglasses out of his jacket pocket. He looked at them for a moment, and then placed them on the table at his side.

"Negative thoughts that arise in your mind need to be pushed out right away. It's just like when you drive through a puddle and splash mud on your windshield, you need to turn on the wipers so you can see. At first, it can be difficult to keep negative thoughts out of your mind, but just like anything, it gets easier with practice.

"Some days are more difficult than others," continued Rama. "So, on those days, it's important to do something that will inspire you. *The Dhammapada* is a wonderful book to keep with you and read whenever you need a little lift. Or if you can't stop what you're doing to read, take a minute to focus on your heart chakra. Your heart is the center of happiness and balance, and by focusing on it without thinking, you can open yourself to the light and power of the universe.

"What we practice and experience are not common occurrences for most people. The miracles you've witnessed are just examples to show you that what you've learned to believe growing up may not be all there is to life. Miracles are meant to inspire you to look at the world with an open mind. It's important to realize, however, the real miracle is the light that manifests itself during meditation. Things in your life may not work out the way you want, but as long as you continue to meditate and be mindful, you'll be able to see and experience light.

"Remember, practicing yoga, which is what we do, is about finding harmony within," said Rama. "If you expect things in the physical world to work out the way you want you'll only frustrate yourself. You have no control over other people, only control of yourself. Yoga is not about creating harmony outside of yourself. It's about finding union with Light. It's an inner study."

Rama then put on Zazen and asked us to meditate. I closed my eyes for a moment, and then gazed towards Rama on the stage. I watched breathlessly as his form changed into a dark-skinned man with a black beard and hair. A wave of nostalgia passed over me as the face began to look familiar. A thought passed through my mind saying, *That time doesn't matter anymore. How far can we take it today? What can we do with it now?* Then I saw him as a fierce and mighty warrior who was going off to battle. Tears began to well in my eyes as I realized I would never see him again as that being. I continued to push the thoughts out of my mind and watch the gold light emanating from the stage. The light began to fill my being, strengthening me and revealing to me the beauty inherent in the universe.

I left the hall that night determined to live in the state of balance Rama had described. I wanted to find that peace not only while meditating, but also during the day at work and in the evening at home with Melony. I doubted if Melony and I would ever be as close as we were in high school, but after that night, I was willing to take a shot at being friends again.

A SECOND INVITATION

The mind is its own place, and in itself
Can make a heaven of hell, a hell of heaven.
-Milton

A few weeks later, the phone rang unexpectedly in the middle of the night. I picked it up on the first ring, knowing somehow it was for me.

"Hello!" said Rama in a cheery voice, sounding as if it was mid-morning rather than 3 a.m.

"Hi," I answered, struggling to wake up.

"Your roommate keeps showing up with an interesting proposition. I ignored her at first, but psychically, she's been using all the correct etiquette, so she does know what she's doing. Now, you have to understand that this is her idea."

"O.K.," I mumbled, trying to figure out what Rama was talking about.

"If I work with you two together, it can be a very powerful combination and move you both into a higher awareness. You can use each other's energy as a catapult. I think it will work, but it's your call.

You've known her for a long time, so is she for real, or is she just playing games?"

"Honestly, I don't know, but I want to say she's serious." I knew I was risking the relationship I had with Rama by involving Melony, but I also missed her desperately and wanted to share my life with her once again. Living with someone who acted like a stranger just wasn't fun for me.

"Are you sure?" he asked, giving me the option to exclude her.

"Yeah, let's see what happens," I answered, confident something good would come out of bringing Melony to Rama's house.

"All right," said Rama, betraying nothing in his voice to tell me whether or not I had made the right decision. "Wake her up and explain the situation. All of this has been on the psychic level, so she'll probably have no idea what you're talking about, which is fine. You don't need to tell her about that part since it will only confuse her more. Just tell her I've invited you both to come down and take care of the house while I'm gone. Being at my house will clear you out and help your meditations, in case you haven't already noticed. Why don't you both take the train out here tomorrow and we'll see how we get along."

I knew my two previous visits to Rama's house had benefited my life in a number of ways. Meditating at his house was a thousand times easier than in my apartment, and when I returned home, things with work clicked into place. Overjoyed I would be able to share this unique gift with Melony, I bounced across the hallway to wake her up. She lifted her head and asked me if the phone was for her.

"No, not exactly. That was Rama," I blurted out, searching for the words to explain Rama's invitation.

"What?" she answered, rubbing the sleep from her eyes.

"On the phone, that was Rama," I continued, my heart racing, knowing I'd have to tell her the whole story. "You know how I've disappeared a couple of times?"

"Yeah." Melony eyed me as if I was making up a story to impress her.

"Well, I went to Rama's house. And remember the guy that called and you thought he was angry?"

"He was angry," interrupted Melony forcefully.

"No. He wasn't. That was Rama too." Melony's eyes dropped as the truth sank in. I paused for a moment, and then continued, "He's invited you to come with me to his house tomorrow. Do you want to go?"

Her eyes lit up like a child's on Christmas morning. "Really? Oh my god!" she whispered. "Yes, of course."

"Good," I replied with a smile. "We have to leave around seven, so we should get some sleep."

As I stood up to go back to bed, Melony gave me a big hug, reminding me of the closeness I felt when we were kids.

Early the next morning, we packed our bags and walked through the snow to catch the train to Rama's house. Melony fidgeted in her seat, trying to contain her excitement. All morning she had asked me what to bring and what to expect. I told her what I could, since I really didn't know what was going to happen once we made it to Rama's house.

We took a cab from the train station and walked up the driveway to the house. I felt like an experienced tour guide taking Melony to the local Enlightened man's house. The whole situation seemed so ludicrous to me. Only a week ago, I wasn't sure if I'd ever talk to Melony about anything more than the household bills, and now I was taking her to see my most treasured friend.

The Scottie dogs greeted us first with yelps of hello. Rama left the door open for us, where I instructed Melony to leave her shoes. Rama came bounding down the stairs from his room when we stepped into the kitchen.

"Hi!" he said, complete with his usual grin.

We both greeted him, and he led us to the guest rooms. I felt more in control of myself than the last time I had been there, probably because I was comparing how I felt to Melony's uneasiness.

"Since you were here first," Rama said to me, "you get to pick which room you want."

"I like the purple room," I answered, walking with my bag into the small bedroom.

"So that leaves you in here," he said to Melony, leading her into the orange room with the lotus carved on the bedframe.

After we unpacked, Rama took us out for lunch at an Italian restaurant that had recently opened. Melony and I spent most of the meal giggling, trying our best to appear comfortable around Rama's intense energy.

Back at the house, when Melony got up from the couch to use the bathroom, Rama told me, "There's no sense in competing with her."

I looked at him blankly, knowing there was nothing I could say to defend myself. I had been trying to keep Rama's attention with idle chit-chat, while Melony had been doing the same.

"You two are completely different in terms of the dimensions you access," he continued. "She pulls more from the power chakra, while you deal more with the artistic centers of the heart. That's what makes it interesting for me. Try to understand that you complement each other. There's no conflict having you both around, unless you make an issue of your jealousy."

I nodded in agreement, trying to control my emotions. I wanted Melony to benefit from being around Rama, and I knew I had to make room for her if we were going to see him together.

"All of the dimensions are separate planes – they don't mix together. All of these dimensions are contained within you, but you tend to pull on certain ones, while she pulls on others."

I pictured in my mind a layered cake, stretching into infinity. After I told him my vision, he laughed and asked if I was hungry.

We meditated late into the night, sending me up to a new high I had never before been able to reach. Rama was right, meditating with the three of us together did have a strong impact that I could use to go further.

In the morning, Rama told jokes over breakfast and coffee, sending us both into hysterics. I hadn't laughed so hard since high school when all of my friends would get insanely drunk. This time, however, I didn't need any drugs or alcohol to feel high.

"But on a more serious note," broke in Rama, "you both need cars, right?"

"Yeah," I answered for the both of us hesitantly.

"And you need to go to computer school to learn the basics, right?"

"Yes," said Melony confidently. She had been talking about earning her certificate in computer programming since she arrived in New York. I was interested, but didn't take it very seriously since I was already working with computers.

"Well, I can help you out with this, but you'll have to agree to take care of things for me when I ask. You know, like watch the house when I travel, and maybe some typing or housework. Nothing major, but it has to be an exchange. Does that sound fair?" Rama looked at us sincerely.

I couldn't believe what I was hearing. I didn't have the money for a car, and I knew computer school would teach me the things I needed to know about programming to get out of the help desk area. It sounded like the deal of the century, but I was still nervous about accepting anything so big, even from Rama.

"Yes, definitely," answered Melony for the both of us.

"O.K. I'll give you each some money for cars, but you have to promise to have a mechanic look it over before you buy it," said Rama. "It should last you for a couple of years, so make sure you have it checked out. Too many people are out there just waiting to rip someone off, especially a young woman with a handful of cash to spend. And start looking into the local schools for a certificate program; something about a year long. There should be a few different schools to choose from. Do some research and let me know what you've found."

We spent the afternoon watching movies before Rama took us to the train station. As we were leaving his house, he handed us each $2500 in cash to buy cars. I looked at the crisp one-hundred dollar bills, wondering why he would keep so much cash in his house.

"We can call it a loan, if it makes you feel better," said Rama as I picked up my bag and prepared to head towards the Range Rover. I smiled weakly, still in shock that he was buying us each a car.

At the train station Rama reminded us again to have the cars checked out by a mechanic, even if they looked great. He also said we should find our passports, because he may need us to travel with him some time.

"If you travel with someone, people are less likely to notice you," he said by way of explanation. The train whistle sounded, so we said good-bye and boarded the train with smiles stretching from ear to ear.

THE ISLANDS

Heaven means to be one with God.
-Confucius

In the middle of March, Rama called to invite Melony and me on a trip to the Caribbean. He suggested we drive down to his house the night before the flight, since there was a storm warning.

We left Westchester late Wednesday night in the middle of a heavy storm in Melony's Honda Civic. The snowflakes swirling in front of the windshield gave the impression that we were cruising at warp speed in a Star Trek movie. Neither one of us could believe our good fortune as we sped through the snow with ease, while other cars were sliding off the road.

Early the next morning, a limo arrived to take us to the private Lear jet Rama had rented. He had taken care of every last detail, setting everything up perfectly. On the jet, he was a gracious host, offering us food and drinks, and even socializing with the pilots, to make sure they were comfortable. Not once did he flaunt his wealth or power. Instead, he simply made it a point to have fun with every moment, always aware of how the rest of us were feeling.

Once we were in the air Melony fell asleep and I had the opportunity to talk to Rama alone.

"You're angry that she's here," he said decisively.

I couldn't argue with him about it. Even though we were friends again, I was extremely jealous of Melony. The way she dressed, the way she held herself – she seemed to do everything better than me, and I hated it.

"You have to realize you wouldn't be here if she wasn't. This would just be too intense for either one of you alone. Do you understand?" asked Rama, his eyes riveting me to my seat. "This is a very unusual situation. Normally, I would have taken an intermediate student, not a new student."

I nodded in agreement, realizing I was blowing the trip before we even touched ground.

"I know it's really stupid to feel..." I started to explain before he cut me off.

"Right now you have a choice. You can either wallow in your jealousy and have a terrible time, or you can get above it. Push yourself to a new level," said Rama, looking me dead in the eye.

"You have to keep reminding yourself," he went on, "that you wouldn't be here if it wasn't for her. Just get that through your head, and you should be fine."

I nodded my consent and he lifted his gaze from me. As I resolved to move past my emotions, I felt something shift deep inside me.

❀ ॐ ❀

On the first island, we stayed at a private resort in a bungalow, which consisted of a large suite, two one-bedroom studios off to the side and a private swimming pool. All of this was situated on top of a hill, providing us with a majestic view of the Caribbean Sea.

When I woke up early the next morning, the whole island was surging with life. A green and black hummingbird danced among the fuchsia blossoms as the wind swished through the trees. Birds hid in the branches chirping while yellow butterflies glided through the air in an elaborate ballet.

The absence of the noises of the modern world amazed me. During my meditation there was no need to block out the sounds of passing cars and screaming children. My thoughts had never been easier to quiet. As soon as I sat down to meditate, joy washed over my being as the colors of the universe danced before me like the hummingbirds going from flower to flower. I pushed past my petty desires and fears that lingered from the States and saw a vision of a mountain rising before me. A wide path curved around with a gentle incline, while another path went straight up to the peak. The thin path stretched up over the boulders on the edge of a craggy cliff, seemingly treacherous yet strangely brilliant. I was drawn towards this narrow and steep path, and could not turn back once I had begun. It was difficult at first to gain my footing, but it became easier with every step as my confidence grew. I kept moving towards the peak of the mountain, until everything dissolved into clear light.

Rama had told me once Enlightenment costs everything and I knew at that moment I was willing to pay. Nothing I had ever known could measure up to even the small amount of ecstasy I had found in meditation. No amount of pain could keep me from seeking that light.

"Rama," I said later in the day as we sat by the pool, "the more I think about the occult world, the less I know. Just when I think I understand something, a new concept pops up and I get more confused."

"Well it's not as easy as it looks," he answered, watching the waves in the bright blue sea. "If it was easy, everyone would have it figured out, right?"

"Yes, I know," I complained. "There's just so much I don't know. I used to think I knew a lot from your seminars, but that's hardly anything compared to the things I'm seeing now."

"What were you confused about, besides life in general?" he asked, ignoring my whining.

My mind went completely blank. I had been reading the book he had just finished writing about his adventures of snowboarding in the Himalayas where he met his master. The book had opened up so many concepts; I didn't know where to begin. I still wanted to know everything, but I didn't know what questions to ask.

He looked at me, waiting for an answer. Then he continued, "You were just reading the Fwap book, so why don't you ask me something about that."

I scanned my memory for ideas, and finally asked, "What's the difference between karma and free will, and how do you know when you're acting on one or the other?"

"You just read about it, so tell me what you doped out from the book," he answered, putting the question back in my lap.

"Well," I began slowly, "karma is like a groove in a record that you're on, due to what you did before, kind of like a track that you're following. And free will is a well that you can draw from to get off of that track. But how do you know which one you're acting on?" I insisted again.

"Yes, that's right. Your karma is composed of everything you've done and thought in the past, including your past lives, up to this moment. It's like a road you've paved for yourself. With karma, you keep following the patterns of your past. You can draw on free will to change your karma, like you can draw water from a well, but that takes energy. Free will is always there as a choice, whereas your karma just keeps rolling along," he explained.

"So was it your karma or your free will that brought you on this voyage?" continued Rama with a smile.

After pondering the subject, I figured that since I didn't use my free will to make him invite me, logically, it had to be the other. So I replied, "My karma since..."

He laughed and said cuttingly, "Your karma? What do you think you did in your past lives to get you to a place like this with an Enlightened master? Do you have any idea of the amount of lifetimes of meditation – we're talking thousands – the amount of work involved..." I could feel my face go red with embarrassment. Obviously, I had completely missed the concept about karma. "Do you really think you deserve to be here? Have some humility, would you? You're riding on my karma, not yours."

This last comment left me completely bewildered, but he didn't seem willing to discuss the subject any further.

The next day, we took a ride down to the shopping area. I slipped into tourist mode, and soon I was lackadaisically strolling along, not paying much attention to anything except the merchandise in the store windows. Melony also fell into this carefree mood and nearly walked into a couple crossing the sidewalk.

On our way back to the miniature Jeep Rama had rented, a car sped towards us. I slowly drifted to the side of the road. Melony, however, was caught up in looking at some purses in a window.

"Move your ass, soldier!" commanded Rama.

Melony, startled by his voice, jumped out of the way of the car with only seconds to spare. Her eyes popped open with fear as she looked to Rama.

"You can't be walking around spaced out in a world like this," he reprimanded, looking at both of us. "This little island may appear safe, but the people who come here have power and are searching for more. That's how they got the money to be here. They'll feel the power that comes from your association with me, with Enlightenment, and they'll want some of it. So if you don't stay sharp and aware, you'll get completely trashed out.

"This isn't a game," he emphasized. "This is real. So you had better start paying attention to what's going on, or else you're going to end up hurting really bad. No one is going to be there to save you, so learn to take care of yourself."

I could see fire flash in his eyes as he warned us again, saying, "People are killers. You're playing with the high rollers now, so don't forget it."

By the time we arrived back at the resort, the mood surrounding us had lightened, but the seriousness of our situation never diminished. We were sipping cappuccino by the pool when Rama brought up the subject again.

"Tantric Buddhism is very complicated," he said softly. "We're dealing with more power than either one of you has ever been exposed to, and you have to learn how to handle it. This pathway to Enlightenment has been called the razor's edge because it's an extremely difficult road to walk. If you direct the energy towards light, you can move to higher states of awareness very quickly. But on the other hand, if you let yourself just hang out, it's really easy to go down just as fast.

"With this amount of energy, you can't just sit on it. You have to do something with it, or else you'll find yourself caught up in some pretty weird places that may not have even been your idea. Not all occultists are interested in Enlightenment. There are plenty of people out there who are just interested in power and domination. Stop living in fantasy land and take a good look at the world someday. People are angry and in pain, and you have to work very hard to get above it."

"So self-discovery is really about self-control?" I asked.

"Yes. Control, control, control," he repeated. "But remember, you can't control other people. You can only control yourself. Just stay aware of where your mind wanders, and keep your attention pulled in when you go out into the world. You don't have to be paranoid; just pay attention to what's going on around you."

On our last day on the island, Rama sat in a chair by the pool, with the expression of one who was planning something. Curiosity soon got the best of me, so I pulled up a chair next to him and asked what was going on.

"On the day of travel," he began, glancing at both me and Melony, "Your astral body is already at the place you're going to. Since your attention is focused there, you can see what it's going to be like. This way you can be prepared, or if you sense something really dangerous, you can re-route your journey. What are you feeling?" asked Rama. "Don't think about it, just say what you feel, even if it doesn't make sense to you."

"I've felt really anxious all day," I said. "Earlier, I kept thinking I had to rush off to someplace, but then I realized I didn't have to go anywhere. So I figured I was picking up on somebody else."

"Okay, that's good," he commented. "Come on, Melony, you have to participate too."

"It feels really heavy," she answered, gesturing with her hands as if she were trying to hold a large weight in the air.

"OK. So where's it coming from?" asked Rama, looking at each of us in turn. "What are we feeling?"

I shook my head to indicate that I didn't know.

"What you're feeling is danger," he said after giving us a few more minutes to discover it on our own. "This is what danger feels like. Now, what's it coming from? Is there something in our route that's going to go wrong? Or is someone just trying to throw us off?"

Puzzled by this last remark, I looked at him expectantly.

"People will do that, throw you off, because for some reason they may not want us to go to that other island. So that's the question. Are we feeling something that might happen, or is it someone screwing around with us?"

"Well," I said, "before I felt like it was someone pushing me to go, so maybe it's coming from someone else."

"Yes," replied Rama. "That pushing sensation is a good clue, and you're probably right. But from now until we arrive on the other island, you'll want to stay aware of what your body is feeling. Things can always change at any moment, so you've got to keep up with it."

In the evening, we made it to the second island without incident. Upon arrival, however, our limousine was not there, nor did they have any record of our reservations. While Rama took care of the transportation, Melony and I stuck together in the dingy airport. Fortunately, the wait was not too long before a car was sent for us.

Once we were inside the limo, I felt more comfortable than I did standing in the airport. But soon, I began to feel a thick, stifling energy surrounding me. As I tried to avoid being sucked into it, I started feeling as if I were sitting with some very heavy drug dealers. I had to pull up my will power to remain relaxed and calm, in spite of the leftover confusion and anxiety I felt from the previous passengers.

Melony sat on my left clenching her fist over her heart unconsciously.

"Just relax," said Rama softly to Melony. "Don't be so nervous. You have to just flow with it. Things don't always work out the way you planned. It's not a big deal."

Melony forced a smile and placed her hands loosely in her lap. I could feel her stress, not only from the car itself but also from Rama calling attention to her nervousness.

When we arrived at the house, a large woman wearing an apron smiled as she greeted us with a hot dinner of salmon and fried plantains. A homemade lemon chiffon pie topped off the meal before she cleaned the kitchen and went home. Exhausted from the journey, we each found a room and went to sleep.

First thing in the morning, we jumped into the ocean outside the back door of our rental home. The plant life and fish were clearly visible in the shallow water, and the sea itself felt alive as I swam among the gentle waves. After swimming, we sat on the porch with our morning coffee.

"So what's going on?" Rama asked me with a curious tone.

I looked at him vaguely. I didn't understand what he meant and I felt slightly dissociated.

"What are you feeling?" he asked again. "You're not smiling, and you're feeling something that I'm not. See, she's not smiling," he said to Melony. "She's not usually like this in the morning, is she?"

"No, she's not," agreed Melony.

I didn't feel quite myself, but I had decided it

was just because I was tired from traveling.

"We all have different levels of perception," explained Rama, "so I always pay attention to how others react, as well as to how I feel. Sometimes the people I'm with will pick up on something I don't notice, like now. You're feeling something that's not affecting me, so what is it? What do you feel?"

"I feel like I have to keep looking over my shoulder, like something or somebody is threatening me," I began slowly as I tried to isolate my feelings of discomfort.

"So you're feeling danger, right?"

"Yes, but it's not like yesterday at the other island. I can feel it inside me instead of outside."

He looked at me and everything went gold. I felt as if he were scanning my being, looking right into my soul.

"You're feeling the people. You're a white woman on a predominantly black island, where they work hard for not much. So you're feeling the hostility some of the people put out, and you feel vulnerable because you're a woman. The energy of this island is very strong, and everything is intensified, since you're in my aura.

"It's good to know what you're feeling because then you can deal with it," he continued. "Your body alerts you to danger. It's a survival mechanism you can use to your advantage."

During my morning meditation, my body shifted gears and finally relaxed into the new environment. Somehow, I had attuned myself to the energy of the island so I was able to blend in and enjoy my stay.

As the sun set, we had dinner at a quaint

restaurant called the Lighthouse. Our waitress was exceptionally kind and friendly. With every action, she expressed a genuine desire to be helpful. Rama spent some time talking to her about the island and the Caribbean while she was at our table. The shine in his eyes told me he appreciated how this woman was treating us.

I discovered that night Rama can change a person's life just by holding him or her in his mind in a certain way through the use of occult power. By the end of the evening, the waitress seemed to be an entirely different person. Her smile was brighter, and she walked with a lighter step. Her aura was smoother, and she plainly looked happier. Rama had changed her life during our meal, although she'd probably never know why her life suddenly seemed so much brighter.

I imagined Rama would say it doesn't matter if she knew or not that she had been touched by the light of Enlightenment. I thought about the time I was told by a friend that life's greatest heroes often go unsung, and I knew Rama was one such hero. Even though he called this particular trip a vacation, he was constantly working by spreading light and teaching me and Melony a deeper level of understanding of Tantric Buddhism.

Swimming the next morning, I turned and noticed that I was very far from the shore. I didn't really care, because I had always been a strong swimmer, and I was enjoying the feeling of suspended animation I got from floating in the water.

"Don't go too far out," called Rama at that exact moment from the beach. Amazed at how he was forever on the watch for me, I swam closer to the shore.

Later on, he explained to me in a very caring tone, "Don't go too far from the shore unless someone is with you. The current can pull you out to sea very quickly, and if you get a cramp, you probably won't make it back to shore. Have you ever had a cramp in the water?"

"No," I confessed. "I've had them when I go running, but not while swimming." In my mind, I thought I was immune to swimmer's cramps.

"They can hit you quite unexpectedly, even if you've never had them before," continued Rama, reading my thoughts. "So it's better to have someone close at hand who is a strong swimmer."

When he looked me in the eye, my thoughts stopped and I knew he was alluding to more than just swimming in the ocean. In my brief time of studying with him, I had learned a little about moving through different dimensions. Lately, I had been pushing myself, perhaps a bit too far without a proper guide.

In the afternoon, we left the house to rent some snorkel gear. On the way to the shop, Melony became unreasonably tense and nervous.

"What are you so uptight about?" Rama asked Melony, who was sitting next to him in the front seat of the car, fiddling with her fingernails.

"I don't know," she replied meekly, shaking her head from side to side.

"Well, figure it out," demanded Rama. "We work together here. Your moods affect us as well as you. It's obvious that something is wrong, so talk about it and deal with it."

"I guess I'm afraid," said Melony, staring blankly into the distance.

"Well, yeah," agreed Rama with a sarcastic laugh. "Now, what are you afraid of – going snorkeling? It's just like swimming underwater, except you can breathe. If that's all it is, it's no big deal. Don't be embarrassed. You have to overcome your fears someday."

Melony squirmed uncomfortably in her seat as Rama threw a side-long glance at her after pulling into the parking lot.

"Figure it out," he stated emphatically as we got out of the car.

In the rental shop, Melony seemed to relax a little, thinking she was off the hook. Rama decided we should have lunch at the picnic area, and sent Melony to order the food from the beach front grill while I took care of the drinks. Once seated, Rama continued his interrogation.

"So, what is it?" he asked, sitting across from her at the picnic table.

Melony shook her head slowly, staring down at the cracks in the table. Rama continued the pressure until she said quietly, "It's probably because someone held my head under the water." Her voice quivered, as if what she was saying was self-incriminating.

"Yeah," laughed Rama, "that would do it." His tone became softer and more serious when he asked who had done it.

"My father," she barely whispered, with downcast eyes.

"Don't be ashamed," replied Rama. "Look at me," he said gently, but she refused. "Look at me," he repeated, the power reverberating in his voice.

She looked up with pain in her eyes, glancing at me and then back at Rama. The proud, strong woman I had known since high school turned into a frightened child in front of us.

"Tell us about it," he continued casually. "It's the past, so it can't hurt you. But if you keep it locked inside, then he still has a line into you, and he's making you relive that moment every time you try to pull away from him. He can pull on that line any time he wants to, giving him power over you. Was it once or repeatedly?"

"He would usually throw me in the shower, but that time the kitchen sink was full of dish water," revealed Melony hesitantly.

"Okay, so the time in the sink, did he push your head under and hold it, or did he do it over and over?" asked Rama, trying to get Melony to recapitulate the scene.

"He pushed my head down, first for just a second. Then he did it again, but held me down longer." As she spoke, a layer of the past fell from her like a piece of worn out clothing.

"Abuse happens to everyone, in one way or another. All these people here," he said, glancing around at the people on the beach, "have been hurt emotionally, physically, or psychically. Don't feel bad about what happened. It's not a unique thing for anyone. The world is a violent place. You just have to work through it, and try to find balance inside yourself.

"When I was a kid," explained Rama, "my dad used to push me around constantly. One day when he told me to do something, I just flat out refused. It wasn't because of what he wanted done; it was the years and years of him pushing me. So I said I wouldn't do it. I was a teenager, tall and lanky without much muscle mass. And he was a big man. Slam! He punched me and asked again if I was going to do what he told me to do. I got up and said no. He hit me again, and I did the same thing. I just kept getting up, until it reached the point where he would have killed me, when he finally walked away. It hasn't been the same since.

"You have to fight, or else people are going to keep walking all over you. To me, it's better to die than to live that way."

Melony nodded in agreement, forcing a smile.

"Don't hold onto that fear!" commanded Rama. "You're still letting him shove you under the water every time that fear holds you back. So you can either move past it, or you can continue to let him have power over you."

Back at the house, Melony donned her gear and disappeared with the fish for hours without complaint. I stayed close to the shore, as Rama had recommended, and kept a watchful eye on Melony's snorkel sticking up through the water. Rama appeared, and beckoned for me to follow him further out. As I swam next to him, the water sparkled and the fish seemed to glow. As we went deeper, my senses sharpened and I glided through the water with no effort. He moved swiftly as we searched for the bright coral the Caribbean is famed for. I followed him closely, but at one point, he disappeared completely, as if the sea had swallowed him.

A thousand thoughts and feelings passed

through me all at once. A part of me felt as if I was moving at an incredible speed, but another part was perfectly still and quiet. Rama returned abruptly, carrying a large orange starfish. Playfully, he chased me with it, until I was laughing so hard I had to take off my snorkel to breathe. Then he handed me the starfish. I examined it's hard, shell-like back and could feel it pulsing with life. Everything was so vibrant swimming with Rama in the ocean. Although I had been in the ocean thousands of times, everything in this underwater world was shiny and new.

The following day, we rented a boat and went to a sandbar called Stingray City. A collection of stingrays swam freely there, and allowed people to feed and pet them. Their skin was soft as silk, rubbing against my legs as they frolicked in the sea. Several times, they wrapped themselves around my ankles, tripping me in the shallow water. I fell, giggling like a little girl being tickled by these magnificent creatures.

As more tourists crowded the sandbar, we left to go to a coral reef the boat driver had recommended for snorkeling. In the water at the reef, I forgot for a while that I was human, and became part of the world of fish. With no one in sight, I dissolved into the water, reaching a point where I felt as if I were flying with no inhibitions. A rainbow of fish swam around the pink coral, ducking into the slender tunnels to hide from me. A long, silver fish swam just inches below me. Proud and vicious looking, he would not diverge from his course in spite of the fact I was twenty times his size. I decided not to follow him, and went back to watching a black and gold fish dance through the coral tunnels.

I looked up from the underwater world to check my position, and saw the others on the boat, waving for me to come in. I swam slowly to the boat, surprised at how quickly time passes under the sea.

At sunset, I went for a run along the beach by our house. Still high from the day's adventure, my legs flew across the sand without a thought. Every muscle in my body shouted with exultation as I pushed myself to go faster. As my feet glided across the sand, I was completely ethereal. The wind blew through me, clearing out residue from the past. With my body and spirit united, I caught a glimpse of what it truly feels like to be alive.

The next morning, we sat together on the porch enjoying the view of palm trees and the vibrant blue water lapping the shore. I tried to absorb it all; the silence and the feelings of the island that made me feel so young and full of life. Rama's aura was glowing softly like the setting sun, sending waves of energy through my body that electrified every cell.

"What do you want most?" he asked quietly.

"I guess to be happy," I answered, trying to formulate in words my deepest desire to be completely free.

"Be more specific," he said casually.

"When I bought my car," I explained hesitantly. "I saw a shooting star as I was saying good-bye to the couple who sold it to me. In the past, I always wished for something when I saw a shooting star, but at that moment, there was nothing I wanted, except to enjoy the beauty of that star as it fell from heaven. And when I went running yesterday," I continued, "I felt so free, like I was an ethereal being flying across the sand. Or in a very deep meditation, when there is perfect stillness. That's what I want, but I don't know how to describe it as a thing that I want."

"So you want to experience a feeling," he said simply.

"Yes," I agreed, but I wanted more than that; I wanted to be that feeling.

"Those are rare moments for most people, because it's a violent, predatorial world. It's not something that's just going to happen. You have to work at it. You have to keep your mind focused on bright and beautiful things while pushing out the negative thoughts that assault you constantly from within and without. You have to be a warrior to get anywhere in this world," explained Rama.

"You have to understand that for most people, the only time they experience any degree of ecstasy is when they have an orgasm or when they're so drunk they can't feel anything. Other people, like us, seek ecstasy in other ways. Something in the subtle-physical composition of certain people makes them strive for power because exerting that power brings ecstasy for occultists. They weren't made that way by anything they did; occultists are just born that way."

Like a light bulb turning on in my mind, I finally understood why I had felt so different from my friends in grade school. The girls I knew always talked about getting married and what kind of houses they wanted, while I dreamed about adventures and traveling to strange lands.

"Life is like an amusement park," continued Rama. "There's one ride at the other end of the park you really want to go on, and that ride may be different for everyone. You know there's one ride that does it for you, and you have to walk through the park to get to it.

"So you're walking, headed for the ride, but there are all of these other rides and games you can get involved in on the way. Everyone looks like they're having a marvelous time, and they invite you over. All of these distractions can keep you occupied, and pretty soon you forget about the ride you originally wanted to go on.

"The trick is to stay focused," continued Rama. "There are a million and one things in the world that can draw you off your path. Just be polite. Say, 'oh that might be fun for you, but I'm going down here.' People can pull you off track only if you let them.

"Like I said before, they call Tantric Buddhism the razor's edge because it is a tricky path to follow. We use everything to advance ourselves spiritually. We live and work in the world, and since most people are not focused on spiritual pursuits, it's easy to get caught in somebody else's ride if you don't stay focused.

"This type of yoga brings up enormous amounts of power, which can lead to extreme egotism or insanity if you don't handle yourself correctly. Not everybody is designed to walk the razor's edge. It takes a certain kind of warrior spirit to control yourself and to keep your mind focused on light while engaged in the battle of survival."

I thought of all the times I had gone along with

some crazy stunt, just because some friend convinced me it would be fun. There really wasn't anything I regretted doing. There were just things I wished I had done if there was more time. Hearing Rama talking about life as if it were an amusement park gave me a new way to look at my options. That analogy made me realize I had to choose every moment and determine if going along with the crowd would get me to where I wanted to be.

On our way home, a lightning storm painted the sky as we flew above the clouds. This spectacular show was the perfect topper for a most empowering trip. We all delighted in watching nature's fireworks display from 40,000 feet.

After eating the snack Rama served us from the plane's refrigerator, he asked us what we had learned from our experiences with him on the islands.

"I learned what it feels like when someone is throwing energy at me as opposed to when I'm reacting to something," I said thoughtfully. "I guess I'm learning to trust my instincts more, as I become more aware of how to read them."

"Yes," commented Rama, "that can be a very useful tool when dealing with the world."

"I found out that there's more in me than I ever realized," added Melony.

"Isn't that great?" said Rama with a big grin. "Everything goes on forever. There's no end to the experiences you can have."

"If you were to go on another trip like this, what would you do different?" he then asked.

"I would keep a tighter rein on my thoughts and emotions," answered Melony.

"Good, because we all feel it, part of being psychic," he replied succinctly.

"I would try to be more aware of what other people need," I answered, knowing on many occasions during the trip I had thought only of myself when making decisions.

"Yes, it's good to try to be more selfless, instead of always focusing on just what you want." As he spoke the cabin inside the jet began to glow and I felt myself go to a higher dimension.

"Preparation is three-quarters of a journey," he continued. "You'll get more out of an adventure by putting yourself in the best possible mind state by working out your body, and by meditating deeply. It's important to take care of all the details before you leave, so you're not held back by thinking about what you should have done. You make sure your life is as tight as possible, because who knows if you're ever coming back.

"And always be prepared for the worst situation that could happen when you travel. That way, when something goes wrong, you don't get thrown off balance. You have to stay on top of things, know what's happening behind your back, especially when traveling in a foreign country where the laws are different.

"Well, now that you've traveled with the Enlightened in a foreign country, can you tell me what impeccability is?" asked Rama, smiling.

"Doing what's appropriate in every situation," I remarked, feeling certain that I was right.

"No. That's not it," Rama replied. "What's it mean to live impeccably?"

"Doing everything perfectly?" questioned

Melony.

"No. There's no such thing as perfection in the world. Perfection only exists in your mind, and the idea of what is perfect is different for everyone. So there's no way to act perfectly, except in your own mind."

Melony and I looked at each other dumbfounded; all of our ideas about impeccability had just been cut down.

"Impeccability is always pushing to move beyond your limits," continued Rama. "Since perfection is really a state of mind, it has limits and cannot truly be impeccability. So that is our goal: to live impeccably, always reaching beyond the boundaries of where we were."

The plane began its descent, but I was so high, I hardly noticed the change in air pressure. When we landed, the March evening air was much colder than the night before in the Caribbean, sending the reality we had returned from our vacation into my very bones. I would definitely miss the house on the beach and early morning swimming, but I knew I had a lot of work in front of me if I ever wanted to get my life in order.

After dinner on the evening we were to leave Rama's house and return to Westchester, I felt extremely excited and happy about my life. Rama leaned against the cabinets, as Melony and I sat at the table, watching twilight turn the sky to a soft shade of violet.

"What are you feeling?" he asked curiously.

"I'm really excited about life, but I also sense some anger," I replied.

"Well, yes," he agreed slowly, "but that's just the

world. This is deeper than that. What is it?" he repeated. "I don't know if you can, but I feel it right around my navel center."

"It's a happy thing," I said after a moment of silently focusing on that spot. "When I focus on it, it makes me smile." I suddenly felt very giddy and wanted to laugh.

"Okay, those are descriptions, but what is it?"

I knew by his insistence he wanted us to figure out what it was, but I didn't know what to call it, and Melony didn't say anything.

"It's a dimension," he finally conceded. "One I haven't felt yet this incarnation. The earth is going through a dimensional shift. It's always changing, but right now there are major shifts as old dimensions close and new ones open. You're feeling a new dimension opening.

"The earth passes through different dimensional access points as it moves through the galaxy. This planet is not only orbiting the sun, but the whole universe is in constant motion. As the earth moves across the universe, different dimensions become available, and it affects life on the planet. The other dimensions are still there, it's just harder to get to them. When a dimension opens up, it's like an open doorway that's available for travelers to pass through.

"This one is a dimension of telepathy. Many more people will become telepathic, so the insanity rate will probably go up in a few years," he said matter-of-factly, as Melony and I giggled.

"It's true," said Rama. "If you don't know what's happening and you start hearing people's thoughts, it can drive you insane. You have to be able to control it, and screen out other people, or else you won't be able to function in society.

"This dimension does feel good. Back in the 50's, America used to feel more like this. It was easier to read in the evening, or just sit and relax."

He pulled a chair up next to me, and we all sat in silence watching twilight turn into night in his yard. I felt perfectly content sitting there, doing nothing but feeling.

"It's like we're watching a video or something, huh?" commented Rama with a laugh.

"Yeah," I agreed, "it's nice feeling, like I can just relax without thinking about having to do a million things."

"When you get back to Westchester, they'll be waiting for you," he reminded me with a sly smile.

SCHOOL DAYS

Teachers open the door...
You enter by yourself
                          -Chinese Proverb

During the first week of April, Melony and I found a local college offering a certificate program in computer programming. After discussing it with Rama, we made plans to begin classes at the end of the month. He said he would pay for half of the tuition, since we would be able to get student loans for the balance. We made arrangements to drive down during the weekend to pick up the money.

This time, I drove instead of Melony, who kept moving around in her seat like a nervous child. She was back to waitressing again, insisting she could make more money doing that than from temporary work, since she couldn't type. I didn't have any help desk assignments, so I picked up jobs wherever I could. I was excited about starting school, because I knew it would get me to play more on my computer at home as I learned how to write programs.

Rama told us he would need us to house-sit in a

few weeks, but there was no reason for us to stay over that night. We went out for a light dinner and discussed some of the projects he was working on with his intermediate students. Once we returned to his house, he gave us each an envelope with money for school.

"When you sign up for school, give them the whole thing, that way, you won't be stuck for tuition later," he suggested with his customary caution.

We talked about the dates that classes started, and he noted the first day of class fell on the day he needed us at the house. Rama explained we should bring both of our cars, and Melony should leave Sunday night so she could go to class. I could get the assignment from her when I returned the following Wednesday.

He sent us home after dinner, and said he would call if there were any change of plans. Once again, Melony seemed nervous on the ride home. I was too excited about starting school to ask why she was in such a weird mood.

Two weeks before we had to go to Rama's house, I had a job offer with a small computer consulting firm. I wanted to accept the position, but didn't know how to explain I would be out of town for a week so soon after starting the job. Finally, I decided to tell him the truth: I had to do some work for the man who was putting me through school. Surprisingly, he replied it was fine for me to take the week off without pay.

Melony and I played cat and mouse on the drive to Rama's house. She chased me down the highway, and then I would chase her. We arrived an hour before Rama had to leave on his trip, so we helped him finish packing. He then sat with us at the kitchen table, going over the phone numbers we may need.

"This is the number to the vet. Vayu has been under attack lately, so in case he has another seizure, call her and call me at the hotel," he explained. Rama stressed once again how the dogs were the most important beings in his life. He had done this every time I had stayed at his house, but this time he seemed more serious than ever.

"Someone's attacking the dogs?" I asked with disgust.

"Yeah. It's hard for them to slam me when they get angry, so they go after my dogs. I have some pretty sick students. And of course, sometimes it's just the regulars from Cult Watch. These people have nothing better to do so they track what's going on with the study. Some of the people in that group used to be my students, and some are the parents of my students." He smiled as if it was a big joke, but I knew from my battle with Melony it was a serious situation.

"Your students do this?" I questioned, more horrified than before. "Why? I mean, you do so much for them."

"Well, sometimes things don't work out the way they think it should, so they take the power I give them and charge it with anger and throw it at me, or in this case, my dogs," answered Rama. "It's pretty stupid on their part. I mean, whatever they throw at me is just going to fly right back in their face. And then they wonder why the world feels so bad. But when they mess with my dogs, that's just sick. I don't see a lot of my intermediate students anymore, and with the ones I do see, all we discuss is business. I've cut down the seminars for them to once a quarter, since that's all they can handle."

After he left, I thought about the times Melony had attacked me and how quickly Rama had recognized what was happening. Obviously, he had experienced the same thing, only a hundred times stronger, with the people he dealt with on a regular basis. I was surprised I didn't realize it sooner. Once again, I had been stuck in my own world, thinking only of myself.

Melony and I didn't talk much during the week at Rama's house. She had been distant since we had decided on a school, so I just let her be. The only time we did talk was when we played with the dogs, or when deciding what to buy for dinner. I spent most of my time writing stories and reading the books I had picked up for school. I had decided to get a head start since I was going to miss the first class.

On Friday night, Vayu climbed into the bed with me and slept near my feet on top of the fluffy comforter. In the middle of the night, I woke up suddenly as I felt an attack from a powerful force. It was much stronger than anything Melony had ever thrown at me. I didn't have any time to be frightened, even though I didn't know where it was coming from. I pulled Vayu into my arms to protect him, and imagined a bright white force field around us both.

A distorted image of some of the intermediate students I had seen at the events flashed in my mind. I knew then they were after Vayu, not me.

"Leave him alone!" I commanded silently as I pushed the force out of the room. There was no one person to direct the energy back towards, so I concentrated on the white light around Vayu and me. I saw the energy hit the barrier and dissipate outside the windows.

The pressure finally ceased, leaving me in a strange state of exhilaration. I realized I had just learned a new way to deal with a psychic attack without causing the damage I had in my battle with Melony. Feeling wired, as if I had eaten too many chocolate-covered espresso beans, I got up and carried Vayu to the living room. Together, we watched *Aliens 3* until I felt calm enough to go back to sleep.

The next day, Vayu had a small seizure, but snapped out of it quickly. The vet instructed me to give him the pills Rama had on hand. When I called Rama in London, he suggested I give him a bath in the sink. After the bath, Vayu was back to his playful self, walking in circles around me as I dried his black fur with a towel.

Melony left reluctantly on Sunday afternoon. She was tempted to stay, since Rama wouldn't be back until late Monday night, but she knew he would be able to feel her in the house. An hour after she was gone, I could feel her pushing me psychically. "Get out of here!" I said out loud, with the dogs looking at me curiously.

My neck started to hurt, and I knew with certainty Melony was back to her old tricks again. I had felt twinges of her psychic attacks during the past month, but kept talking myself out of it, convinced I was just feeling the world. I continued to focus on my computer books and keeping the dogs entertained while waiting for Rama to return.

On Monday, the sun was shining, so I sat outside as the dogs ran across the yard. The salty cold Atlantic kissed the rocky shore as dark cornflower blue waves rolled ceaselessly through Long Island Sound. *Who am I?* The question echoed over and over in my mind as I tried to comprehend the mystery of life. I could never return to the life I once knew before meeting Rama. Those days of drinking in the bar intellectualizing about what I was learning in college were long gone. I was far away from the realization of Enlightenment, but through Rama, I had glimpsed the pure light and ecstasy.

As I sat alone, watching the waves, I knew I was living in a no-man's land of impossible dreams. I didn't have enough power to push through to the other side, and no possibility of returning to ignorance. I could feel each and every cell in my body tingling from head to toe. It's like riding an invisible rollercoaster, I thought to myself, as long as you don't fall out of the cart, it's a fantastic and exciting ride.

Rama arrived home late in the evening and was greeted by the dogs with their chorus of yelps and barks. After scratching each of the dogs, he sat down on the couch and told me about the seminar with his intermediate students, describing the scene as "a fat man going to an island of cannibals."

He took one look at the horrified expression on my face and started laughing hysterically. Between bouts of laughter, he mimicked my facial expression by putting his hands against his cheeks and opening his mouth as if he was going to say "Oh! The horror of it all!"

Despite my confusion, a small smile started to curl on my lips as I began to see how I must have looked to him.

"Don't get me wrong," continued Rama with that I-know-something-you-don't grin. "I love all of my students. They are truly amazing people. When things don't work out the way they expect, many of them still freak out. Old habits are hard to break."

"Yeah, that's true," I replied. My feelings of anger towards the students dissipated when I saw the compassionate way Rama forgave them. I then described Friday night's attack on Vayu and mentioned that I watched *Aliens 3* to calm myself enough to go back to sleep.

Rama simply replied, "That's why I have those movies."

I started rubbing my neck again, and thought of Melony sitting at home alone.

"So now she's really pissed, huh?" said Rama, referring to Melony.

"Yeah, she didn't want to leave on Sunday, but it sure lightened up when she did."

"She needs to go to the first night of class," said Rama. "It will help her in the long run, even though she doesn't see that now. I'm sure it's going to get a bit weird for you at home with her, but just be political. She can't handle the energy right now. She keeps losing her balance and taking it out on you because you let her. So just be cool since you'll need to deal with her in class."

When I arrived home, Melony was hungry for news about Rama. I told her he sent his regards, and we had watched movies until I left for home. I didn't know what to say. I knew Rama had decided not to invite her back to his house, but it didn't seem like it was my place to tell her.

A week later, I was sitting in the kitchen reading my computer book for school. Suddenly, I became distracted by a sense of danger drawing closer and closer, as if someone was stalking me, honing in for the attack. I kept getting up to look out the screen door into the darkness, but nothing was there. I focused harder on my homework, ignoring the question that kept going around my mind: *Why does this person want to eliminate me?* A few minutes later, Melony walked through the door and whispered a hello to me in a sticky sweet voice.

What did I do to arouse such violence from her? I wanted to ask as she wandered around the kitchen and into her room. My body began to ache all over, and I couldn't concentrate on my studies. I tried to read faster and focus harder, but every bone and muscle burned with pain until I left the kitchen for my bedroom and shut the door.

I spoke with Rama at the next seminar. He immediately knew what had been happening with me and Melony. He asked me to deliver a warning to her that she was in danger of losing a lot more than an invitation to his house if she continued the attacks.

The seminar seemed to be the night of warnings. On stage, Rama told us two students, Matthew Hamilton and John King were no longer in the study. They had joined Cult Watch and had attempted to persuade another student into joining them. He warned us they may attempt to contact people to recruit them for Cult Watch, and we should be on our guard.

I gasped as Rama said Matthew's name. Matthew? Of all the people in San Francisco, he had been one of the most devoted. He had never spoken to me in New York, even though I had given him my phone number when he had first arrived, hoping to renew our relationship, but he had never called. Now in a sad way, I was thankful we were no longer close.

Once we were home from the seminar, I told Melony about Rama's message to her. She looked like I had just slapped her when I finished talking. All she could do was say, "I'm sorry," over and over. I felt bad for her, but I knew if I let any of my feelings for her show, I would be the one who was sorry.

INDEPENDENCE DAY

To be nobody-but-yourself -
in a world which is doing its best,
night and day,
to make you everybody else -
means to fight the hardest battle
which any being can fight;
and never stop fighting.
-e.e. cummings

The consulting firm I had been working with revealed to me the darker side of the computer business. Repeatedly the owner left his clients with failing systems while he went to find other accounts. Although I had been hired as a secretary, I provided what technical support I could over the phone, but with my limited skills and no training on the systems I was supporting there was little I could do solve their problems.

The most experienced technician was an over-worked programmer who had no patience for the constant questions. The other technician, who was the main support person, seemed to know less than I did about the clients' configurations. Frustrated by the lack of teamwork and organization, I quit the firm without notice.

The following Monday I hit the phones, calling all of the placement agencies I had been forming relationships with since I had moved to New York. There were no helpdesk or training positions available, so I settled for a temporary position doing word processing.

All week I wanted to talk with Melony about my decision to leave the consulting company, but she was practically a stranger to me now. Working in a secretarial position had shaken my confidence. I needed to know if I simply wasn't qualified to handle a consulting position or if it really was the company's lack of organization that had made me leave.

When the grades came out at the end of the school term, I had earned straight A's for the first time in my life. This ego-boost made me realize computers weren't too difficult for me and if I tried, I could land another job in the industry.

As if on cue, a manager at the office where I was temping offered to give me a referral to his friend's computer company. He had been impressed when he overheard me talking about school with another woman at lunch, and said his friend's company was always looking for good help. I wrote a cover letter and faxed my resume to the computer manufacturer, explaining in my letter how I wanted to learn more about hardware.

I went to an interview on Friday, and started as the Chief Technical Officer the following Monday. When the owner neglected to share my title with anyone else in the company, I realized the title was in name only and would carry no weight except maybe on a resume.

During the next two weeks, I learned everything I could about the manufacturing process of computers. I started off on the assembly line with motherboards and hard drives, and soon I had the entire process from work order to completed machine down pat. The foreman of the factory seemed a bit worried when he commented that I had learned in two weeks what had taken him a year and a half to pick up. I reassured him I was not interested in his job, and told him I was there to learn everything I could.

After the initial excitement of my new job wore off, I began to experience an intense case of insomnia. No matter how many sleeping pills I took, I couldn't sleep more than an hour or two. Once again, I wished I could confide in Melony but there was nothing left for us to talk about. I hadn't slept for nearly two weeks, and was lying in bed around 2 a.m. writing in my journal when the phone rang. I knew instantly it was Rama. I had been practically crying for him to call me – I couldn't take the stress anymore.

Rama invited me to his house, telling me to try to get some sleep before driving down the next morning. After attempting to meditate, I finally drifted off into a light sleep. The next day I stopped at a payphone to call in sick to work, and by the end of the conversation I knew I had lost another computer job.

Rama asked me what was going on as we sat in the deli near the center of town. I couldn't explain other than telling him I hadn't slept in weeks. I wanted to point out the cause of the stress, but there was nothing physical I could point to other than Melony and I didn't want to blame her. Frustrated, I told him I felt like the world was crushing me, and I didn't know how to fight it.

"Even though life hurts sometimes, you have to be tough," said Rama, his tone cold and distant. "Now, obviously you're a complete mess, so pull yourself back together. I can't do it for you."

I wanted to tell him I knew I would bounce back, that it would just take a little time, but I couldn't get the words out. I knew if I started talking, I would break down in tears. I silently picked at my spinach lasagna, as he continued to tell me to snap out of my depression.

I had been riding high for nearly two years, ever since I had met Tara and had begun meditating regularly. Now, I was crashing hard and couldn't stop, even though Rama was sitting right next to me.

We spent the afternoon running errands, and then settled down on the couch to watch a few movies. Rama seemed to be ignoring me, and I didn't feel like talking, so I stayed lost in my own thoughts.

The next day, I felt a little better, but my mood was still down. Rama seemed angry with me and my attitude as he drove to Blockbuster to return the movies.

"You can't stay this way. You'll wind up pushing a shopping cart down some alley if you're not careful," he warned like a worried parent.

Tears began to well in my eyes as I struggled to speak, but I couldn't tell him what I needed because

I didn't know. I wanted someone to hold me and tell me that everything would be all right until the feeling passed. I knew I couldn't share an apartment with Melony anymore, but I also knew it was only part of the problem. Even though she was slamming me psychically, a part of me still wanted to maintain a friendship with her.

I needed to focus on my life and let her go. Not wanting to cry in front of Rama, I swallowed my tears in silence with downcast eyes.

In the afternoon, Rama gave me money so I could move into my own apartment. "If it was me, she would be the one moving out," he said before sending me home.

I thanked him for the money and left knowing it would be hard to tell Melony I was leaving. Rama was right about keeping the apartment. If the rent wasn't so high for our place, maybe I would have told her to move out. The thought of her having no place to go and of me finding another roommate made my stomach turn, so I faced the fact that I needed my own place. As I drove home, I began to feel lighter than I had in weeks.

I knew Melony would be angry about having to find another roommate, so I made arrangements to stay with Tanya while I looked for a place I could afford on my own. Tanya and her roommate were having their own financial difficulties, and I felt like a burden in their presence. I needed to find a new home fast, but I couldn't find my focus.

Unexpectedly, Rama called my voicemail to ask me to dog sit. I arrived at his house in a much better mood than the last time, but I was completely exhausted. He told me to try to relax while he went to London on a business trip. "Take the dogs for a walk around the yard. Being outside will help clear you," he suggested before leaving.

Late in the night, I fell into a deep, dreamless sleep and didn't wake up until nearly dinner time the next afternoon. The dogs were upset about being inside all day, but forgave me once they had a biscuit and a long run around the yard.

The rest of the week, I wandered around the yard, admiring the lush trees and bushes surrounding Rama's house. He had planted a variety of flowers that were all blooming, creating the appearance of an English garden, complete with a bench in one corner of the yard.

Between sitting on the dock watching the water behind his house and lying under the shade of a Japanese maple, I was rejuvenated. By the time Rama returned from London, I felt like a person again, as opposed to the bundle of raw nerves I had been when I arrived.

When Rama pulled in the driveway, I was wide-awake and ready for the dogs to begin barking. I helped him drag his suitcases in the house as the dogs cried for attention.

"You look a lot better," he commented as he scratched Vayu's ears.

"It's surprising what sleep can do," I answered with a smile, feeling the effects of standing next to him. It always amazed me how just being near him could shift me into a higher state.

"Yeah, that's very true. I know, I've been through it too," he continued compassionately. "These people just don't know when to quit. Obviously, it's not just the intermediate students attacking us; it's a whole psychic network of people.

"But," he added with flourish, "I had a great vision on the plane back from London. I saw a new way to teach yoga. It's business!"

Rama was extremely excited about this new insight, but as he talked, I became more and more confused.

"You see, for years, I've made energy available to my students, and asked them to use it for their practice of meditation and in their careers. But they need something more structured; this free-form style just isn't working," he said. "So if I change the program to focus exclusively on business, people can still benefit from working with me, and I can teach business based on spiritual principles. We could have companies run and staffed by Buddhists. Since everyone would be practicing meditation, the energy level would stay high. You won't have to go work for someone who is going to drain you, because everyone at the company would be getting their energy from meditation."

Swept up by his enthusiasm, I toyed with the idea of leaving the world of temporary jobs to work for one of his companies.

"So, Enlightenment comes to corporate America. Wow," continued Rama, entranced by the vision he had on the plane. "I'll announce it on the Fourth of July. On Independence Day, I'll no longer be a spiritual teacher."

I tried to hide my disappointment. I had never met someone as inspiring as Rama, and now he was giving into the attacks by doing what they wanted him to do: give up teaching meditation.

"I know this is probably difficult for you to

understand," he continued. "But shifting the focus of the program to business is the best for everyone. You see, I've already taught them the basic meditation techniques. There's no need to sit and repeat the same thing over and over. The more advanced concepts are very difficult to comprehend, and most people need an analogy they can relate to. The students also need something to focus all this energy on, so business is the perfect medium for Americans. The whole idea behind Tantra is to incorporate spirituality into every aspect of your life. The students haven't been doing this. Instead, they throw the energy around, as I'm sure you can testify to. By changing the program, the energy has a structure to flow into, making everyone more productive."

The next morning I my initial troubled feeling about this change in the study intensified. I was doing well in school, but I was not at the level in computer science I should have been by that time, even with my past assignments. And now with Rama talking about having us work for one of his companies, I knew I was nowhere near ready.

The more I thought about working for him in the computer field, the less excited I felt. Anxious about wanting to remain his student, I decided I would have to work harder regardless of how disappointed I felt about the project.

"I guess I need to do more push-ups to get myself motivated," I said with a weak smile as I picked up my bag when it was time to leave.

Rama looked at me compassionately with his bright blue eyes. In a soft, clear voice he returned, "It's not about doing more push-ups. That's not going to make a difference. There's no need to turn your life into a struggle. You just need to quiet your mind and get your ego out of the way. Just be yourself. There's really no way you could be anything you're not."

As I drove down the tree-lined road the sun poked through the leaves. I had the feeling Rama had been trying to tell me something about my long-term goals. I wanted to work with him as a writer, but computer school and work had driven that dream underground.

In my free moments, I filled notebooks with pieces of stories, but I didn't know how to pull it all together. I finally pushed away my worries and smiled, confident Rama was right. I just needed to keep meditating and the light of Enlightenment would guide me along the way.

At Tanya's house, I poured over the newspaper until I found an apartment I could afford. With the changes in the study less than a month away, I had to push myself into high gear to have a stable place to call home. When I went to look at the apartment, a smile crept across my lips as I recognized the place. The apartment I had seen in my dream the night I decided to leave San Francisco had materialized before me.

The next few months, I spent most of my time alone, working on my computer studies and writing. Rama continued to hold seminars, but instead of discussing the magic and mystery of Enlightenment, he talked about the different companies we could work for on a commission basis.

He discussed sales techniques and

recommended a series of business books before stepping back to let his intermediate students take the lead in teaching us how to be successful business people.

I joined a few study groups, but nothing we did sparked my attention in the same way talking about spirituality did. I wanted to see Rama, so I continued to attend the seminars, hoping for a chance to hear him talk about Enlightenment.

In October, Rama called me to house sit once again, so I canceled my latest temporary assignment and made the journey to his home. I had received a couple of job offers in the past few months, but not wanting to be unavailable to house sit for Rama, I had declined. I convinced myself I could make more money and have much more freedom in taking short contracts than I would if I worked for someone full time.

Before leaving for his trip, Rama asked me when I was planning on getting a real job.

"Well, if I take an extra class next term, I should be done with my certificate in the spring," I answered, avoiding the real question.

"Just a target date. What do you think? Next spring then?" he questioned, trying to get me to nail down a specific date.

"Yeah, I guess," I said, not so sure I wanted to get a permanent job.

Satisfied, Rama finished packing for his trip and left me alone with the dogs. Later in the evening when I thought about the conversation, I realized Rama's questions were his way of hinting I needed to start thinking seriously about my career, instead of just taking it as a temporary arrangement.

Before I left Rama's house, I made a vow to myself I would find a real job to help me move faster in my computer career.

Three weeks later, I joined a large consulting firm, where I learned the inside business of dealing with clients and contracts while increasing my technical skills.

Between school in the evenings and a heavy workload during the day, I had less and less time to focus on the study. The projects I had started with Rama's other students ended, and I didn't take the time to get involved with any new ones. Slowly, I began to drift out of the relationships I had formed with the students and started to form new friendships at work and school.

In December, I ran into Anthony on my way to the office. He was working just a few blocks away, but planned to leave soon to move back to California.

"I've learned so much from Rama," he told me over lunch, "but I think I've gone as far as I can on this path. I don't really hang out with anyone from the study anymore. There just doesn't seem to be anything for me."

"Yeah, I know what you mean," I said wistfully, almost wishing I had the strength to make that decision. "Sometimes I really want to leave too, but I have nowhere to go. I like the seminars, but I keep getting the feeling I should be somewhere else. I can't tell if it's the other students pushing, or if it's me."

"Really? I thought I was the only one who felt like that. Why don't you just take a leave of absence? Rama has let other people leave the study and then come back. I was just in San Francisco on business, and I know I need to live there."

"What are you going to do there? Did you see any leads on work?" I asked, excited by the idea of moving back to California.

"Actually, the company I'm with right now has offices all over the world, so they'll let me transfer. And maybe I'll go back to school. I was about to go into law school before I met Rama, but I put that on hold to study with him."

When Anthony left, I wished him the best and asked him to stay in touch through email.

To celebrate the holidays, Rama threw a few parties, bringing everyone together to dance wildly to techno music. The evening he rented the Guggenheim museum in Manhattan, I wanted to tell him how proud I was about my job with the consulting firm. Fortunately, the dancing never stopped and I didn't have the chance to tell him before realizing how egotistical I would have sounded.

During the next few months, I began having financial problems. No matter what I did, I seemed to be constantly broke. Coming up with the money for tuition at the seminars was suddenly a stressful chore, but I was determined to make it to Rama's classes.

I felt my life spinning out of focus. I thought I needed to be at the seminars, but I didn't have the money or energy to attend.

I asked Tanya if she was having any problems, and she told me "nothing more than usual." Rama's plan to focus exclusively on business had been working for most of the students. Many of them had doubled their income in the past few months, however, I felt like I was falling behind the crowd. Rama no longer called me to house sit, and I was not inspired to work any harder than I was to make money.

In February, I couldn't cash my check in time to make it to the seminar, so I decided not to attend. Tanya reminded me I could always pay tuition in March, but something inside me had already given up on the seminars.

I thought of Anthony striking out on his own, and wondered if it was time for me to do the same. I remembered Rama once told me to follow my heart and it would lead me to wherever I needed to go.

As I sat home alone that night, I asked myself if I should continue to attend the seminars, and it became clear it was no longer appropriate for me. I had been fighting my true feelings, but at last I knew it was time to explore new horizons.

During the next few months, I could feel the power in my life and I knew how to use it. I finished the certificate program with straight A's and joined a writer's group that met once a month. I found an Aikido class and began to relearn the basics of the martial art. At work, I demanded a raise and was rewarded for making a stand.

Soon after I became the technical writer for my team at work. Through experience, I learned how to structure user guides and technical manuals that were informative and easy to read.

Once in a while, I missed talking to Rama, but as long as I meditated, I could feel the light. Somehow, Rama had helped me reach a place where I could see and act upon the infinite number of opportunities available to me at any moment. Whenever I began to doubt the connection I had with Rama, he would appear in a dream to remind me he would always be my teacher.

One night I woke startled from a deep sleep. I remembered the dream with vivid clarity: I had been severely injured and was lying in a hospital bed paralyzed from the neck down. Rama came into the room and moved his hands over the top of my body, filling it with brilliant gold light. We smiled at each other as I began to move my arms and legs; the movement caused me to awaken in the night.

The next day in Aikido class, we practiced throws over the shoulder. My partner used his strength instead of the technique, and as I flew up over his shoulder I twisted the wrong way and landed on my head. My neck crunched, and I rolled up into a half-lotus seated position. Everything went gold and I could not move for several minutes. I felt my sensei and my partner crouching next to me with concern. As I came back to consciousness, I knew Rama had healed me.

Tanya and I remained friends, but most of the others I knew from the study faded away with time. Later that year, when Rama published the book I had read in the Caribbean, Tanya told me about a book signing he was having for *Surfing the Himalayas*.

At the book signing, hundreds of students formed a long line that snaked through Barnes & Noble on Wall Street and onto the sidewalk. The people I recognized greeted me with an open heart, and I felt once again I had found my tribe. My path at that time led me to solitary practice, but it was comforting to know these like-minded people existed in such great numbers.

From my place in line, I noticed Melony on her way out of the store. A wave of anxiety passed over me as she caught my eye and headed towards me. I pushed my expectations of another battle away, determined not to slip into my old habits. I had changed since our last confrontation, and it was reasonable to think she had put our history behind her as well.

Melony greeted me with warmth, telling me how happy she was to see me again. I told her about my work as a technical writer, and she mentioned she had entered the world of database design.

The war between us was over. We finally stood together in a space of mutual respect, one strong woman meeting another. We parted without exchanging phone numbers, both of us knowing if we ever needed to find each other it wouldn't be too difficult.

The line moved slowly forward, as hundreds of people stood in front of Rama one by one. When I handed Rama my copy of *Surfing the Himalayas* to sign, he smiled with genuine delight, making me feel like a close friend. At that moment, I knew anything I could dream was possible for me now.

Rama had taught me the things I needed to know to continue on my path without him holding my hand every step of the way. I wanted to thank him for teaching me how to live a bright and beautiful life in this world, but there were no words to express my gratitude. I smiled at him, knowing he would continue to guide me on my journey to Enlightenment, whether I saw him the physical world or not.

As I headed back to my client's office to finish writing a user guide for their latest software release, Rama's words from a seminar that seemed ages ago rang in my mind: "Meditate. Practice mindfulness. And do whatever it is that makes you high while you live your life." The subway door opened at Grand Central, and I smiled, knowing I was finally on the right path for me.

EPILOGUE

Spending time away from Rama's study program allowed me to solidify my solitary practice. It also gave me time to write this book and move forward in my computer-consulting career. Although I did not see Rama physically, I still felt him and the energy of Enlightenment every day when I sat in meditation. I also often felt the energy pulsating through me during ordinary moments at work or hiking in the woods. My entire practice strengthened at this time.

When Rama changed the program once again, this time adding the study of various books to his work in the corporate world, I began to sporadically attend the seminars. Whenever it felt right, things would come together and I would find myself at the lecture hall with all the other students.

At one meeting, the student at the attendance desk tried to block my entrance, since I had not been participating regularly. I pushed through the opposition and after speaking with Rama's secretary, I was allowed to go in and never faced that problem again.

With winter came one of the worst snowstorms in New York's history. The snow fell so heavily they actually closed Manhattan. The next day I took the train to work, which turned into a 4-hour ordeal both ways. A few weeks later, my friend in San Diego invited me to visit, and while basking in the sunshine I realized it was time to move back to California.

My plans were complicated when I fell in love with a man who lived near my parents' house in New England. We began a long-distance relationship across 200 miles, and I knew I could not handle keeping the relationship going if I moved across the country. We talked, and when I told him I planned to move to San Diego, he decided to join me. Early the next winter, we moved.

Once again, things seem to magically work out in all aspects of my life. My client permitted me to telecommute from home, if I agreed to travel to New York once a month. Nearly every month when I traveled to New York, Rama would just happen to be having a seminar.

This continued until April 1998, when I received a call at my hotel room notifying me Rama had left the body. All during the night, in my grief, I felt his presence sitting in the chair by my bed. A memorial was held at the Greenwich Hyatt, where we filled the banquet hall with flowers. His lawyer announced that before he died, Rama had set up the Frederick Lenz Foundation to help promote American Buddhism. It was still in its early development, and no one knew what it would come to be.

Over the next few months, I posted a poem on a website a Rama student had set up to allow us to connect. With the formal student organization and study program gone, we were on our own.

On the www.RamaLila.com website, I signed my poem "Jenna in OB" with my email address. This went against everything I had been taught about protecting my privacy on the internet.

A week later, a woman who studied with Rama in the 1980's contacted me, and I learned we lived only ten blocks from each other. As we talked, more and more similarities of ridiculous proportions were uncovered, right down to the names of our spouses and the cars we drove. The whole thing felt like a setup orchestrated by Rama.

A powerful friendship formed, and we co-founded Dharma Center to share the teachings we had learned from Rama.

Fifteen years later, we still feel Rama in our lives leading us deeper and deeper into Enlightenment. Although the body we knew him in is long gone, He is still very much alive. I am so happy you have met him through this book. Don't be surprised if you notice him appearing in your life through dreams, or through play with clouds, birds, or butterflies. Keep your eyes open for odd little incidents that make you smile, and you may find yourself entering the same worlds of power and worlds of light he revealed to me.

STARDUST BIRD

A Story for Rama Students – Past, Present, and Future

A bird made of stardust stretches across the heavens, bridging the gap between all the worlds. Upon noticing the suffering radiating from a small blue planet called Earth, the bird gazed upon the world. The Rama shook and shimmering feathers fell to the surface. Feathers of a million different colors and sizes floated down, and out of these feathers, a million people would be born to shine the Light.

One pure white feather grew in the heart of a man named Frederick. As the feather rooted deeper, he became the mouthpiece of the Rama. Tirelessly he taught and gathered thousands of students all around the world. Each of them also held a feather within their hearts. They called him Rama, not understanding. They saw Light pour from his body, and learned to sit in the silence of no-mind. In that timeless, spaceless place, they merged. He showed them the view of the stardust bird stretching between all the worlds. Over and over, he carried them deep into the Light.

A few students began to know the way, so they showed others, and they all began to shine.

When the body of Frederick died, some became lost because they did not understand. Others vanished into private practice, seeking to disappear into the Light. A few continued to teach and share what they knew in their hearts. New students, born with feathers in their hearts, found their way to the others.

The Rama continued to speak to all who held a feather, communicating in a million different ways. Factions formed, all insisting they heard the true voice. Confusion reigned until finally, they sat in the silence of no-mind.

In that timeless, spaceless place, they merged. One by one, each opened their eyes, saw the feather in their hearts, and knew: We are Rama.

ABOUT THE AUTHOR

Jenna Sundell, ordained as a Buddhist monk of the Rama Lineage, began offering meditation classes to the public in 1994 after receiving a teaching empowerment. In 1998, she co-founded Dharma Center, where she teaches Practical American Buddhism. In an effort to share meditation with as many people as possible, she writes and offers classes throughout the country.

Look for her upcoming book, slated for release in 2014, *Peace with Pain: Your Guide to a Joyful and Productive Life in a Malfunctioning Body.*

You can learn more on her blog: www.jennasundell.com and find her on Facebook.com/JennaSundell and Twitter @jennasundell.

www.dharmacenter.com

www.jennasundell.com

Made in the USA
Monee, IL
02 December 2019